# Praise for Tom,
## His Books, and His Work With Writers

"Tom Bird is not only a teacher-mentor, but he's also a guide to listen to the heart of God." Dorothy Wilt, <u>Nursing the Spirit</u> (American Nurses Association)

"It was a struggle to sign up for your workshop (my husband and I are both currently unemployed), but I followed my gut instinct and went for it! Tom, it was worth every dollar to me, more than you could imagine. Thank you again for your help! I have been searching to regain my identity as a writer, and you helped me to do this. Thank you, Thank you, Thank you! I now have the confidence to pursue my dreams, and I don't feel so alone or so weird anymore." Ingrid G., Boca Raton, Florida

"I had the pleasure of meeting Tom in Erie, PA, on Saturday and am almost done with his books. They are awesome! ...very well-written and easy to follow; so far, so good!" Doug, Erie, Pennsylvania

"I have read numerous books on writing, publishing, and selling creative works from authors such as William Goldman, David Trottier, Skip Press, and the list goes on. While the information from these experts has been invaluable, I would put Tom Bird's unique voice right up at the top of the heap." Debbie D., U.S.A.

"I attended one day of your most recent visit to Emory University here in beautiful downtown Atlanta. Unfortunately for me, I had serious motorcycle plans (like, buy one) for the rest of the weekend and could not attend the other two days. You are wonderful! You really 'connect' with your audience and have such a great sense of humor. You explained the degree of difficulty in getting published but didn't dwell on that point. Instead, you inspired! I could feel the excitement around me when the evening was over. The audience of all ages and degrees of education was enthused about continuing their dream of writing." Jackie, Atlanta, Georgia

"I work long hours at my daytime job, so I had to get my writing in *during early morning and late evening hours. Within a three-week period, I wrote 80,000 words."* **Lorraine J., Roswell, Georgia**

*"I am delighted to tell you that <u>Fractal Murders</u> has been honored by being listed on the Fall Book Scene Mystery Top Ten list. This is a great honor as selections are made based on nominations from independent bookstores nationwide."* **Mark Cohen, U.S.A.**

*"Yes! Tom, I just received a 'please send us your book and submission package for review' on The Golden Ones!"* **Carole, Virginia**

*"I'm still getting positive replies from agents on my query letter package. I got yet another one during the week of the 13th."* **Dorothy, Scottsdale, Arizona**

*"Thank you for that gift. Thank you again for your commitment to spread the good word in such a positive, joyful manner."* **Vicki, New Mexico**

*"I was a student of yours, University of New Mexico class, April 2001. I'm a little slow, but determined. After months of writing and diligently reading your encouraging newsletters, I sent out 26 query letters. So far, I have received two invitations to submit proposals and sample chapters. I'm working (with excitement) on getting these out."* **Leo, New Mexico**

*"I received your books recently. This is my second set, as I took your course at Old Dominion some years ago and loved it. I wrote two screenplays and even obtained an agent for one of them."* **Debbie D., Virginia**

"<u>Letting Your Heart Sing</u> is doing very well, and I'm thrilled with my new life. Not only is the book touching peoples' hearts and inspiring their souls, so are my talks. Last June when the book came out, I quit my accounting job, and now all I do is write, give talks, coach people, and lead workshops and Bliss Groups all over the country. My schedule is a little fuller than I anticipated, but I love it. After the book had been out about four months, the tide turned, and I no longer had to bang on doors, send e-mails, or make phone calls to book dates for book signings or talks. Word of mouth traveled fast, and people and organizations began vying for my time! Yesterday, I met Rosie O'Donnell and gave her a book (who *knows where that may lead). And a member of one of my spiritual groups was a producer with the Oprah Show for seven years. He LOVES the book and is doing everything he can to help me get the book on Oprah. I can hardly keep up with the correspondence from readers and keep getting asked, 'When is the Workbook coming out?' I am currently working on it and expect it will be out next year. I don't know how this happened, but <u>Letting Your Heart Sing</u> made its way into a women's prison, and they have started a Bliss Group there, and are using the tools in my book to change their lives so that when they get out they do not have to return to a life of crime. Instead, they can live the lives they were always meant to. I can't tell you how much joy and gratitude that brings me. So, Tom, in ways you can't even imagine, the work we did together continues to transform lives everywhere. I refer people to your web site constantly, so don't think I'm not thinking about you, I am. And I can't thank you enough for helping me fulfill my deepest heart's desire: to share my stories in such a way as to inspire others to follow their heart's desires, so that they too can experience the indescribable joy that comes from letting their heart sing." Deborah Tyler Blais, student and author of <u>Letting Your Heart Sing</u>*

*"A few days ago I had the pleasure of signing with an agent who has recently sold other house and home books to the major publishers and who lobbied heavily to sell my book as well. She already has two of the majors, McGraw-Hill and Simon & Schuster, interested in seeing more about this book, so I am one step closer to seeing <u>Best Ideas for the Built-In Features That Will Make Any Home Extraordinary</u> on bookstore shelves in 2004. Thanks for all your wonderful help and encouragement!" Carol, Sedona, Arizona*

*"I am most grateful to have attended your workshop in Mesa last week. I have been writing almost every day, have started with the index cards, and have briefly sketched the seven books I have wanted to write for years. One book (<u>Woven Hearts: Poems Celebrating Our Connectedness</u>) is written and spiral-bound, and my novel is flowing. (That dam can't hold me back anymore!) Thank you for presenting the most exciting workshop I have ever attended! Robert Frost said, 'I am not a teacher, but an awakener.' Indeed, you are an awakener!" Sherry B., Mesa, Arizona*

# THE SPIRIT OF PUBLISHING

### THE ULTIMATE GUIDE FOR GETTING WHATEVER IT IS THAT YOU WRITE INTO PRINT NOW!

## Tom Bird

Sojourn, Inc.

Copyright © 2001, 2003, 2004 by Thomas J. Bird

All rights reserved. No part of this work may be reproduced or transmitted in any form by any means, electronic or mechanical, including photocopying and recording, or by any information storage or retrieval system, except as may be expressly permitted by the 1976 Copyright Act or in writing by the publisher.

Requests for such permissions should be addressed to:
Sojourn, Inc.
P. O. Box 4306
Sedona, Arizona 86340
www.Sojourninc.com

Bird, Thomas J.
   *The Spirit of Publishing: The Ultimate Guide For Getting Whatever It Is That You Write Into Print Now!*

Layout: J. L. Saloff
Cover: Manjari Graphics
Fonts: Century Schoolbook, Capitals, President

ISBN: 0-9707258-7-6

*Fourth Edition*

# About the Author

Tom Bird was only twenty-six years old when he dropped to his knees and made his urgent plea. "If you show me how to connect with the artist that is so desperately trying to get out of me, God, I will always make time to share this secret with others," he stated.

Two nights later, Bird was awakened from a sound sleep with the solution he had requested.

A publicist with the big league's Pittsburgh Pirates at the time, but an aspiring author at heart, he immediately put the plan that was shared with him into play. His efforts met with instant results. Within two weeks, he landed the services of the publishing industry's most renowned literary agent, who sold the rights to his first book to the third largest publisher in the world only a few weeks later.

True to his word, Bird began offering his secrets shortly after. Over the last two decades, Bird has made over 2500 teaching appearances at over 100 of the country's top universities and colleges, including: Duke University, the College of William and Mary, the University of Texas, Ohio State University, the University of Nebraska, New York State University, and Old Dominion University. Over that period of time, he has shown tens of thousands how to connect with and then direct the artist within us all.

Besides that, Tom has penned 13 books, and his byline has appeared in dozens of publications. His books include: *Willie Stargell* (Harper & Row, 1984); *KnuckleBALLS* (Freundlich Books, 1986), coauthored with big league Hall of Famer Phil Niekro; *Hawk* (Zondervan, 1996), written with future Hall of Famer Andre Dawson; *POWs of WWII: Forgotten Men Tell Their Stories* (Praeger, 1990); *Fifty-Two Weeks or Less to the Completion of Your First Book* (Sojourn, 1990); and *Literary Law* (Sojourn, 1986). He has also contributed to such distinguished magazines and newspapers as *Parade, USA Today, The American Banker, The Pittsburgh Post Gazette,* and *Sail.* In addition, he has also recreated the experience of his revolutionary workshops in an interactive computer program for writers, *The Author's Den.*

Tom's continued success has led him and his work to be featured in *USA Today, The New York Times, The Los Angeles Times, The Chicago Sun-Times,* and over 100 other publications. His work has also been featured on most of the nation's top news and interview programs including "The David Letterman Show," "The Tonight Show," "CBS Morning News," "The Today Show," "The Charlie Rose Show," "CBC," and "The 700 Club."

And now, just for you, Tom has taken all of the secrets behind how he and his students have connected with their Artists Within (AW) and shared them in this book.

To learn more about Tom and
his innovative programs,
or to potentially sponsor one of his
retreats or classes in your city or town,
feel free to either call his office
at 928-203-0265 or check out
his website at:

www.TheSpiritOfPublishing.com

# The Spirit of Publishing / Tom Bird

# Acknowledgments

This book would not have been written without the assistance and encouragement of so many. First, thank you to my students and friends who pushed me to write this book. Thank you to Jamie Saloff, who diligently formatted, corrected, and refined my work, and to Evelyn Still for copyediting. Thank you as well to Manjari on coming through on the cover for this book on such short notice. Thank you most of all to God for providing me with the following insights and information, as well as the means to distribute it to those who need and want it.

# Table of Contents

**About the Author** - - - - - - - - - - - - - - - - - - - - - - - - -VII

**Acknowledgments** - - - - - - - - - - - - - - - - - - - - - - - - -XI

**Introduction** - - - - - - - - - - - - - - - - - - - - - - - - - - - -1
    About First Connecting With and Then Following Your
        Inner Guidance - - - - - - - - - - - - - - - - - - - - - - -4

**Step One: Discovering What You Really Want to Write** - -7
    Words of Others Who Have Taken This Route - - - - - - - - - - -8

**Introduction** - - - - - - - - - - - - - - - - - - - - - - - - - - - -9

**Chapter One: Eleven Essential Days** - - - - - - - - - - - - - -13
    One - - - - - - - - - - - - - - - - - - - - - - - - - - - - - - - - -13
    Two - - - - - - - - - - - - - - - - - - - - - - - - - - - - - - - - -14
    Three - - - - - - - - - - - - - - - - - - - - - - - - - - - - - - - -16
    Fears of Failure - - - - - - - - - - - - - - - - - - - - - - - - - -16
        Fears of Not Deserving: - - - - - - - - - - - - - - - - - - -16
        Fears of Lack: - - - - - - - - - - - - - - - - - - - - - - - - -16
        Fears of Loss: - - - - - - - - - - - - - - - - - - - - - - - - -17
    Fears of Success - - - - - - - - - - - - - - - - - - - - - - - - -17
        Fears of Demise: - - - - - - - - - - - - - - - - - - - - - - -17
        Fears of Exposure: - - - - - - - - - - - - - - - - - - - - - -18
        Fears of Loss: - - - - - - - - - - - - - - - - - - - - - - - - -18
    Four - - - - - - - - - - - - - - - - - - - - - - - - - - - - - - - - -18

## TABLE OF CONTENTS

Five ---------------------------------------- -20
Six ----------------------------------------- -21
    Freedom of Choice: ------------------------- -21
    Creative Freedom: -------------------------- -21
    Financial Freedom: ------------------------- -21
Seven --------------------------------------- -22
Eight --------------------------------------- -22
Nine ---------------------------------------- -23
Ten ----------------------------------------- -23
Eleven -------------------------------------- -26

## STEP TWO: UNDERSTANDING YOUR PUBLISHING OPTIONS ---- -27

## INTRODUCTION ------------------------------- -29

## CHAPTER TWO: YOUR OPTIONS ------------------ -31
Conventional Presses ------------------------ -31
What a Book Publisher Is Supposedly Thought to Do --------- -32
    Publish Your Book -------------------------- -32
    Manage Your Cash Flow ---------------------- -32
    Edit Your Book ----------------------------- -32
    Distribute Your Book ----------------------- -33
    Market Your Book --------------------------- -33
    Design the Artwork for Your Book ----------- -34
    Copyright Your Book ------------------------ -35
    Represent the Specialty Rights for Your Book to Other
        Publishing Options --------------------- -35
    Literary Agent Needed ---------------------- -35
    The Advance -------------------------------- -36
    The Amount of Money You Actually Receive --- -37
    The 90-10 Reality -------------------------- -37
    Credibility -------------------------------- -39
Self-Publication ---------------------------- -40
    Former Drawbacks of Self-Publishing -------- -40
    Expensive ---------------------------------- -41
    Less Than Worthy Alternatives -------------- -41

## TABLE OF CONTENTS

    Distribution - 42
    The Self-Publishing Solution - 43
    What a POD Press Does Offer - 44
    What a POD Press Does Not Offer - 44
  What Does It Cost to Go POD? - 46
    Formatting - 46
    Cover Design - 47
    Editing - 48
    Legal - 50
    Promotion - 51
    POD Costs - 55
    Credibility - 56
    Choosing the Right POD House - 56
    Distribution - 58
  Articles, Short Stories, and Poetry - 58
  The Ultimate of All Solutions - 59
  Checklist - 60

### STEP THREE: THE INITIAL CONTACT PHASE - 71

### INTRODUCTION - 73

### CHAPTER THREE: DODGING THE THIRD CRITICAL ERROR MOST WRITERS MAKE - 75

### CHAPTER FOUR: THE WRITER'S RESUME: THE QUERY LETTER PACKAGE - 79

  The Query Letter - 81
  The Five Elements of a Fiction Query Letter - 82
  Sample Fiction Query Letter - 85
  The Five Elements of a Non-Fiction Query Letter - 86
  Sample Non-Fiction Query Letter - 88
  Salutations and Such - 89
  Credentials - 89
  This Decision Is an Easy One to Make - 89
  Snail Mail - 91

## Table of Contents

### Chapter Five: Whom to Submit Your Work to and How — -93
- Let the Author Beware — -93
- Where to Find That Right Agent — -95
- How to Choose That Right Agent — -96
- Finding a Literary Agent for Your Book — -99
- Querying Magazine Articles, Short Stories, and Poetry — -101
- Commonly Asked Questions About Query Submissions — -103

### Chapter Six: Collaborative Agreements — -107
- The Two Collaborative Routes — -107
  - Ghostwriting — -107
  - Co-Authoring — -108
- Duties and Restrictions: Paragraphs 2, 6, & 11 — -109
  - Title of the Work: Paragraph 3 — -110
  - Approval by Celebrity: Paragraph 4 — -110
  - Preservation of the Celebrity's Rights: Paragraph 5 — -110
  - Ownership of Copyright: Paragraph 9 — -110
  - Income: Paragraph 10 — -111
  - Arbitration: Paragraph 14 — -111
  - Death and Disability: Paragraphs 15 & 16 — -111
  - Literary Agent: Paragraph 18 — -111
  - Governing Law: Paragraph 21 — -112
- Sample Collaboration Agreement — -113
- Some Excerpts From Tom's Good News Newsletter — -117

### Step Four: Submitting Your Work — -119

### Introduction — -121

### Chapter Seven: How to Submit Your Writing — -123
- Submitting Your Book Idea — -123
  - Reviewing, Evaluating, and Most of All Standardizing Your Agent Responses — -123
- The Submission Package — -124
  - Author Bio — -125
  - The Overview or Synopsis — -126

## TABLE OF CONTENTS

    The Chapter-by-Chapter Sketch - 127
    Sample Work - 128
    The Proposal Package - 128
Sample Non-Fiction Proposal Package - 129
The Submission Package for Adult Fiction - 136
    Elements of a Submission Package for Adult Fiction - 136
The Submission Package for Children's Books - 136
    Elements of a Submission Package for a Children's Book - 136
Sample Synopsis - 137
    Including a Sample Illustration - 138
Preparing to Create the Submission Package — An Energy and Timesaving Exercise - 139
Sample Brainstorming Letter - 142
Sending Your Submission Package - 144
Deciding Upon a Literary Agent - 144
Commonly Asked Questions About Submitting Your Writing - 145

## CHAPTER EIGHT: LITERARY AGENT AGREEMENTS - 147
    A Time-Related Agreement - 147
    A Project-Related Agreement - 148
    Open-Ended Agreements - 148
Other Contractual Considerations - 149
    Expenses - 149
    Hidden Costs - 149
Sample Literary Agreement - 150

## CHAPTER NINE: CONTRACTUAL OBLIGATIONS FOR SHORTER PIECES - 153
Getting It in Writing - 153
Elements of a Magazine Contract - 154
    Money - 154
    Whether You Will Be Writing on Assignment or Speculation - 155
    Kill Fee - 155
    Payment Schedule - 155
    Expenses - 156
    Photographs - 156

## Table of Contents

    Length .................................................. 156
    Delivery ................................................ 157
    Publication Date ........................................ 157
    Rights .................................................. 157
  Informal Magazine Agreement ............................... 159
  Formal Magazine Agreement ................................. 160

### STEP FIVE: THE SALE PHASE .................................. 161

### INTRODUCTION .............................................. 163

### CHAPTER TEN: THE SALE ..................................... 165
  Longer Material ........................................... 165
  Book Publishing Agreements ................................ 169
    An Advance Against Royalties Earned ................... 169
    Payment of an Advance ................................. 170
    Royalties ............................................. 170
    Deadline .............................................. 171
    Copyright ............................................. 171
    Paperback Considerations .............................. 171
    Book Club Rights ...................................... 172
    Subsidiary Rights ..................................... 172
    Foreign Rights ........................................ 172
    Movie Rights .......................................... 172
  Articles, Short Stories, and Poetry ....................... 173
  Commonly Asked Questions .................................. 174
  A Closing Note ............................................ 176

### APPENDIX .................................................. 177

# INTRODUCTION

If you are like any other red-blooded human being, everything you have heard about getting published likens it to climbing K-2 on your elbows. Then, even if you somehow happen to miraculously arrive, the best you can hope for is to freeze to death in poverty or to die tragically from some embarrassing, sexually transmitted disease and to be buried in a common, unmarked grave. Is it any wonder, then, that it has been so difficult for you to apply yourself as diligently to your writing as you have to other tasks in your life?

I am not here to tell you that you can't make it as a published author. I am not here to tell you that you have to suffer to become the published writer your heart has fought for you to become.

I know how you feel, for I was there once myself. I listened to all of them as well, from English teachers to college professors to actual authors. I read all of the books, hundreds of

*"If you have anything really valuable to contribute to the world, it will come through the expression of your own personality, that single spark of divinity that sets you off and makes you different from every other living creature."*

Bruce Barton

them, and then I ended up frustrated, confused, and angry.

It has been so often said that a person doesn't change until it becomes too painful not to. Out of options, I finally got down on my knees and had a talk with God about how I was feeling and the whole situation, and then I asked for His guidance.

Two days later, all the cobwebs were cleared from my head. For once, I could see the situation clearly. I put into play what I saw. Two and a half weeks later, I landed the services of the publishing industry's most influential literary agent. Six weeks later, the third largest publisher in the world purchased my first book for an amount equal to three times my annual salary.

I started teaching at the college and university level shortly after because I had made a promise to God that if he gave me the way, I would share.

At present, I have appeared before over 35,000 students all across the country, and I have never heard back from any one of the students who was not satisfied with the results. Thousands have gone on to publish.

However, I must warn you, before you move into the meat of this book, that you will probably not receive what you expect. As I have already mentioned, I *do not* believe that one has to suffer first to publish, nor do I believe that it needs to be difficult. In fact, I staunchly believe that it can be easy if we just get the heck out of our own way and ride the inner guidance that has been pushing us to publish in the first place.

As a result of that, you will find the system I share with you to be very exacting and simple, so simple that at first, you may not actually believe that it could be that easy. However, as the

> *"He who hesitates is a damned fool."*
> Mae West

# INTRODUCTION

excerpts and acknowledgments I've included illustrate, all you have to do to succeed is just follow the steps that I have laid out for you.

The first step I strongly suggest you take on your pilgrimage to publication is to reconnect with that Source that led you to want to write in the first place through the exercises of Part I. Once reconnected, riding the flow of your own personal path to success will once again be available; and as long as you stay on the right road, you're bound to get to where it is that you want to go.

My best,

Tom

*"Twenty-four years ago, I was strangely handsome; in San Francisco in the rainy season I was often mistaken for fair weather."*

Mark Twain

# About First Connecting With and Then Following Your Inner Guidance

## A Testimonial: Jamie Saloff

"Perhaps the biggest, most significant thing to have happened is as follows: I was feeling very harried and felt like I was working nearly 16 hours a day. I felt as if I never left the computer, never got anything done. I was at the breaking point. I have a sense that I must have intuitively cried out for help because God replied.

"One day Tom called, and we got into a long-winded conversation about how things had been going for me. Tom stressed that I needed to make that inner/higher/Godly connection *every day,* before doing anything else, and that I should reconnect at some point midway through the day. I felt that he was right but wasn't really sure how to connect anymore, even though it had been a powerful part of my past.

"I knew that I had once been living in a place where I was connected all the time, but I had lost that somewhere and didn't know how to get back. I tried writing on index cards, listening to music, and a wide variety of things, but nothing seemed to 'click.' I still felt disconnected from my writing self or muse.

"One morning, not long after my talk with Tom, I was exercising with my headphones on. I wasn't doing anything specific, just whatever felt good. I got really caught up in the movement and music. Suddenly, 'ting,' I was in that place where time moved at a different pace, where nothing on the outside mattered because I temporarily rest-

> "There is surely a piece of divinity in us, something that was before the elements, and owes no homage unto the sun."
> — Thomas Browne

# INTRODUCTION

ed within a space of perfect and unconditional love.

"Over the next few weeks, I concentrated on bringing that connection back to where it had once been – and am still – making sure that *every* morning I have time for that all-important personal time.

"Just as Tom predicted, and as I knew from years past, everything else in my life began to pull around into balance. In addition, knowledge began flowing through my heart, my mind, and my pen. Two important things happened as I consistently maintained that connection.

"During one of my connected moments, I was given three very simple steps to help me complete my book. The first was to simply make one index card for each bit of knowledge I wanted to share concerning my book. I started working on them right away, spending no more than about 20 minutes a day writing. I thought I would have maybe 10 to 20, maybe as many as 50. I stopped counting after having opened my third pack of 100 cards.

"Another important thing happened as I continued working forward every day. I had been trying desperately for the past year, year-and-a-half, to find a basic system, set of keys, or steps to go with my book's concept, but they had always eluded me. I had more or less given up until I started connecting on a daily basis again. One day, as I neared the completion of the index cards process, I discovered the book *Mind Mapping* by Tony Buzan. This piece of knowledge came exactly as what I needed, when I needed it. (Tom had always said it would happen just this way.)

"I started mapping out all the concepts I had written on the cards. All I can tell you is that the

*"God is subtle but He is not malicious."*
Albert Einstein

knowledge I received was so mind boggling, so powerful, so easy to understand, that on at least one occasion, I had to stop writing entirely—I was so overwhelmed with thanks and relief, I couldn't continue that day.

"Another synchronistically appearing source that helped me tremendously both in writing the index cards and in making my daily connection was Ira Progoff's book *At The Journal Workshop*. A passage in the Progoff book alerted me to the idea that I wasn't listening for a *voice* per se; I could also write down images I saw, physical feelings I felt, or any memories or thoughts coming to mind as they were probably key to whatever question or situation I might be writing about at that time. This bit of information made mind mapping even more powerful than before.

"Thus I have continued since, spending time each day connecting, mapping, and writing. Everything is going really well. Money, pleasure, and pursuit of my deepest heart's desires are all flowing as they should. I feel happier, more at peace, and on track with my highest purpose. Tom was definitely right, the CONNECTION is the key."

*"Resolve to thyself: and know, that he who finds himself, loses his misery."*

Mathew Arnold

# Step One: Discovering What You Really Want to Write

# 1

**Goal: Avoiding the Biggest Mistake Writers Make**

## Words of Others Who Have Taken This Route

*"I am writing and am telling my story, a great story. I am writing reality, truth, laughter, tears, pain – dammit, I am writing me, me and my feelings. It is a great story that seems to come out easier every morning.... I have accomplished more than I would have ever hoped to in the past two weeks and have successfully thrown out 'overwhelming' from my vocabulary. I am me, stronger than ever, and I love it."* Karen B., Florida

*"I've been writing for over eight years without having completed what I wanted to successfully write. Three and a half months after the Intensive Writer's Retreat, my book is done and a second is halfway finished. The ME that I met head-on in the retreat was set free to write."* Isabella Q., Jacksonville, Florida

*"I wasn't a religious person, but I was very spiritual, and I really wanted to be more than a writer. I wanted to be a channel for God. I just wasn't sure how to do it."* Denise B., Virginia

*"...the combination of steering me towards my own Higher Power as the source, and the hands-on, practical how-to, was exactly what I needed to get up my courage to really DO it. I'm starting to believe that I may actually see this book in print someday. Maybe some day soon."* Dea C., Albuquerque, New Mexico

*"Years worth of crap to get rid of, and I am already breaking through it. And all this in just a couple of days already. For the first time in my life, I really feel that I can realize my dream to write books and be published."* Vicki, Albuquerque, New Mexico

# INTRODUCTION

As with each step that follows, I have chosen to write a separate introduction detailing exactly what it is that will be expected of you.

In this initial section of the book, we will immediately attack what I have discovered to be the biggest mistake that writers make. That mistake, of course, is not really connecting with what it is that drives you to write, a connection you often lose when you sell out to the 'shoulds,' 'have tos,' 'musts,' and the overall conscious responsibilities of life.

Through the following eleven exercises, which are designed to be completed consecutively, that which is currently getting in the way will be removed and you will then be led to reconnect and direct that all-essential inspiration. Your life will never be the same again. I promise.

Of course, if you have already read and put into play my book *Your Artist Within*, you can bypass this section, pass go, collect all of the pats

> *"I just look in the mirror and I say 'God, it's really fantastic, the Lord really gave me something.' So why on earth should I cover any of it up?"*
> Edy Williams

> *"A little less hypocrisy and a little more tolerance toward oneself can only have good results in respect for our neighbor; for we are all too prone to transfer to our fellows the injustice and violence we inflict upon our own natures."*
>
> — Carl Jung

on the back and pecks on the cheek you deserve, and move on over to Part Two.

However, for those of you who are still riding this one out with me, there are a few essentials that are important for you to keep in mind before moving ahead.

**First**, you will need only at most an hour of uninterrupted time to successfully complete each exercise.

**Second**, make sure that the area in which you choose to perform the following is void of potential distractions, including the telephone.

**Third**, it would also be best if you had before you a large, lineless drawing tablet to write on. Make sure that a pen or two are nearby, as well.

**Fourth**, you may choose to use a cassette player to record the following instructions, for use with this and future exercises. You can play them back to yourself, allowing you to focus on the exercises and not be distracted by trying to remember them.

**Fifth**, here are the sequence of actions that I want you to follow to insure you are in the proper state to begin your writing each day:

Begin by uncrossing your arms and legs and closing your eyes, keeping them shut until it is time to open them. If you are at all able, begin breathing in and out through your nose. All of this will allow you to relax.

As you do the above, allow yourself to smile as broadly as you can for about a minute. Then relax, breathing smoothly in and out through your nose. Your mind will clear, and any and all thoughts that could interrupt you from going to that deep, calm space within will leave.

Now, to gain even greater peace of mind and relaxation, take in a nice deep breath and then blow out that breath. After you have done that a

# INTRODUCTION

few times, take in another deep breath, but hold that breath to the count of ten before releasing it slowly while counting downward from eight to one. Then do this again. Take in a nice, deep breath. Hold that breath to the count of ten before releasing it, counting downward from eight to one. This second sequence of breathing will give you the peace of mind you seek, while the first type clears out any and all tension, setting you up for the successful completion of the more gradual sequence.

At any time during this or any other relaxation exercise that you do in this book, if you begin to feel the least bit tense or anxious, or you begin to lose contact with the feeling or image that you had in your mind, breathe in deeply and blow out the breath. Do this as many times as necessary until you regain the necessary calm and peace of mind to do this exercise.

Once you have completed the above steps, let's move on to your writing exercise for Day One.

*"You have no idea what a poor opinion I have of myself – and how little I deserve it."*
  W. S. Gilbert

# The Spirit of Publishing / Tom Bird

# Chapter One: Eleven Essential Days

## One

Begin by allowing your mind and your imagination to recreate for you the time and the place, no matter where or when or how far back, that you first realized writing was something you really wanted to do.

Remember to remain calm at all times. If you need to repeat the breathing exercise on page 10, do so, and then listen and observe where it is that your mind and your imagination take you.

Notice the time. How old were you, and what were the circumstances? What were you doing when this recognition came to you, and what, if anything, caused you to feel as you did? Remember to remain calm. Use the breathing method, if necessary, to remain relaxed and receptive so you can hear, feel, and see why this

> "The last quarter of a century of my life has been pretty constantly and faithfully devoted to the study of the human race – that is to say, the study of myself, for in the individual person I am the entire human race compacted together. I have found that there is no ingredient of the race which I do not possess in either a small way or a large way."
>
> Mark Twain

time, this place, and who you were at the time were so important to you. Drink it all in. Let the image in your mind speak to you. Experience whatever it is that you feel.

What is it that you really wanted to write and why was it that you really wanted to write? Ask yourself these questions. Allow yourself to feel your responses, and then open your eyes, pick up your writing utensil, and allow whatever images and feelings that surface to flow out onto the paper, in whatever shape, size, or design they choose to take. Remember to listen to them and allow them to speak to you in this manner. Remember to perform the breathing exercise listed above if you feel as if you are disconnecting from the images as they speak to you. Don't edit the words or images that come out, don't judge them, or even read them. Allow them to express themselves freely, and just feel and learn from whatever it is that they have to share. Continue to do this until you have filled the paper or until the hour you have set aside to complete this exercise has expired.

Once you have completed the above, you are finished for the day. Wait at least one night's sleep before moving on to the next step.

*"The most important thing is to be whatever you are without shame."*
Rod Steiger

# Two

One of the most delightful aspects about connecting with what I refer to as your *Author Within* or AW, is that doing so comprises not a one-way, but a two-way communication, which means that you can ask questions from this all-seeing, all-knowing part of you and receive images or impulses or feelings that equal responses.

Make sure that your large drawing pad and pen are nearby. Now, let's go back to that special place, time, and space in our minds where we were in the last exercise. Remember to insure that your arms and legs are uncrossed, that your eyes are closed, and that you are breathing in and out through your nose. Remember to use the breathing method which you utilized previously to clear any tension or anxiety that you may feel.

Once you have returned to that special place and time, allow yourself to sink into it, as if you were falling backwards into an easy chair, and then just relax. Take a few of the controlled breaths you used earlier, if necessary, to help you.

With your special time, place, and space waiting for you in your mind at all times, open your eyes and ask yourself the first following question. Then, close your eyes, take a few controlled breaths, feel the response, and then release it onto the paper, in whatever form it chooses to take. Then, repeat the same exact sequence as you move onto the second and third questions, as well. When you have experienced the necessary responses in their entirety, you are done for the day. Remember, though, not to read, edit, or judge any of the replies you receive. Just feel them as they are released.

> *What is the main reason that you feel you don't deserve to further your writing?*
>
> *What repercussions do you fear most about attempting to further your writing?*
>
> *What is the worst possible scenario that could happen to you via your attempt to further your writing?*

*"If you accept limitations, you go beyond them."*
Brendan Frances

# Three

Out of the misconceptions that have been forced down our throats about writing has come a collection of *Fears of Failure* and *Fears of Success* that we now associate with literary success. It's now time to take a look at those fears, but first slip into that most private of all spaces you were asked to venture into on the last two days. After doing so, respond on your drawing pad or on lineless paper with any reactions that may come. Remember not to judge or censor how you feel, just let the inspiration flow. If you feel nothing at all, that's fine too. Just be yourself.

# Fears of Failure

### Fears of Not Deserving:
- *"No one would be interested in what I'd have to say or do anyway."*
- *"Anything that I would try on my own wouldn't work."*
- *"No matter what I do, I always wind up screwing it up."*
- *"I just have a difficult time feeling that I deserve anything good in my life."*

### Fears of Lack:
- *"I'm not smart enough."*
- *"I don't have enough money."*
- *"I'm not attractive enough."*
- *"I'm not brave enough."*

> *"There are hazards in anything one does, but there are greater hazards in doing nothing."*
> Shirley Williams

- *"I'm not dedicated enough."*
- *"I'm not serious enough."*
- *"I don't have good luck."*
- *"I haven't paid my dues."*
- *"I'm not talented enough."*

## FEARS OF LOSS:
- *"I don't deserve to leave those I am with to do what I'd enjoy doing instead."*
- *"My family, or husband, or whomever, wouldn't understand and would abandon me."*
- *"I wouldn't have time for those who matter most in my life."*

*"The man who fears suffering is already suffering from what he fears."*
  Michel de Montaigne

# FEARS OF SUCCESS

## FEARS OF DEMISE:
- *"If I do what I want, I'll be expected to continue doing so; I won't be able to go back to the comfortable position of my past."*
- *"I don't know what awaits me out there."*
- *"I'm afraid that I won't be able to keep up with the pace."*
- *"If I do what I want and succeed, I'll be expected to continue to succeed, and I don't know if I could deal with the pressure."*

**FEARS OF EXPOSURE:**
- *"I'll look like a fool."*
- *"Those closest to me won't understand."*
- *"I'll be attacked."*
- *"People will know more about me than I am comfortable with them knowing."*
- *"I'll be seen as being crazy."*

**FEARS OF LOSS:**
- *"I will lose everything."*
- *"I will lose the structure in my life."*
- *"I will lose the love and confidence of those closest to me."*
- *"I will be overtaken by what I'm doing, and I won't be able to fulfill my obligations to those I care about."*

After you have entered your special muse place and reacted to the above, you are done for the day.

# FOUR

To move successfully beyond the effects of your past, some forgiving needs to be done. Usually that forgiveness takes the form of forgiving others. However, when it all boils down, the one that needs to be forgiven is you, for it was you on a spiritual, soul, or mental level that somehow, and for whatever reason, made the choices that put you through whatever unpleasantries you endured. As you come to grips with this under-

> *"Keep away from the people who try to belittle your ambitions. Small people always do that, but the really great make you feel that you, too, can become great."*
>
> — Mark Twain

standing, it is then that you come to the realization that what you were doing when you were blaming others was projecting what you were not able to face about yourself onto them. So my feeling is that you should just skip all of the unnecessary steps in between and cut immediately to the chase, which is what you will be doing in this exercise. It may take you one session or several. Whichever is the case, remember to stay with it until it has been successfully concluded. Otherwise, you will just wind up wasting time by having to repeat it over and over again later. What does "successfully completed" translate to? In this case, "successfully completed" means until you can perform the following exercise and feel no reaction, at all.

As usual, you will need your drawing book for this exercise.

Use the previous steps to return to the scene depicting the initial time and place in which you realized you wanted to write. However, see yourself as you appear today standing alongside the image of yourself that you usually see in this scene. Then, have your past presence turn to the present you and begin a sentence with the words, "I forgive you for...," and then allow the latter to finish its expression all on its own.

Allow yourself to absorb however it is that you feel, and then open your eyes and allow yourself to release your feelings, no matter how direct or diverse, onto your drawing pad. Remember not to read, edit, or judge. Just allow however it is that you feel to flow. Allow the images and feelings associated with your reactions to speak to you, and cleanse you, from the necessary need of forgiveness once and for all.

After you have done that, go back to the image in your mind. See the two of you standing

*"There is only one success – to be able to spend your life in your way."*
Christopher Morley

there once again and repeat the experience. Stay with this exercise for however many sessions, days or weeks, necessary until your past self has nothing else to forgive you for. When you have accomplished this, you have been released from your past and are ready to move on. But do not turn to the next exercise before then, otherwise you will end up eventually killing your momentum and having to scrap all that you've written up to that point.

# FIVE

With the blockages now removed between you and what you really want to write, it's now time to allow whatever it is that has been seeking to express itself through you to finally be released.

So, go back to your special place. Focus on yourself as you are in that space, and ask yourself the following questions, one at a time, and allow the answers to release themselves on the paper in front of you. This exercise may take you an hour or less, if you choose, or may carry over to several sessions. Either way, stay with it until everything that you have to express has been said.

If, during this exercise or at any other time during any other exercise, any type of personal reaction pops up, repeat the forgiveness drill until your feelings are cleared.

> *What do you want most out of your writing?*
>
> *What are your reasons for desiring what you want out of your writing?*
>
> *What is the most pleasing potential success scenario that could happen to you as a writer?*

*"After a certain point money is meaningless. It ceases to be the goal. The game is what counts."*
Aristotle Onassis

# Six

Below are some typical responses to the questions posed in Step Five. As you can see, they have been arranged in three categories. Read them all over and highlight any that, in general, match your previous responses. If some of your replies fell outside the general design of the responses listed below, list them for yourself on your drawing pad.

## Freedom of Choice:

- *"I want what I want because it's the most enjoyable thing that I can think of doing."*
- *"I want to spend my life doing what I believe is right and putting my energy into something that I feel will make a difference."*
- *"I want to get away from my staged lifestyle."*

## Creative Freedom:

- *"I want to live a creative life."*
- *"I want to spend my life doing something I enjoy."*
- *"I would like to do something that would enable me to share my vision of the world with others."*

## Financial Freedom:

- *"I want to earn enough to do what I want with my life."*

*"Life is either a daring adventure or nothing."*
  Helen Keller

> "Grasshopper, look beyond the game, as you look beneath the surface of the pool to see its depth."
> — Master Po, *"Kung Fu"*

- *"I don't want to have to work if I don't have to."*
- *"I want to enjoy life."*
- *"I want to be able to give myself and my family everything we want out of life."*

# Seven

Relax and go to your special place. Once there, allow yourself to be shown your ultimate goal as a writer. Allow yourself to see actually living it, enjoying it. What are you doing? Where are you doing it? How are you doing it? Describe what you envision in great detail. Begin now.

After you have completed the above, envision where you'd like to be in five years, three years, one year, six months, three months, one month, and one week. Describe each in great detail, and the action plan that comes to you to accomplish each goal.

# Eight

To properly reverse the fears that have kept you from growing and progressing as a writer, it is important that your new writing habits be positively reinforced. But to be able to do so effectively, you must first establish what are appropriate rewards for you.

Thus relax, go to your special place, and then allow an overflowing list of things you like to do, or would like to have, no matter how grandiose, to flow from you and onto your paper.

# NINE

Relax by going to your special place. Once you are there, open your eyes, and look at the list you comprised during your last writing session. Now, divide that list into three categories: small, medium, and large reinforcements or endeavors. These items or rewards are to be used as reinforcements for your efforts expended during the publishing process. Please do not ignore this step, for as trite as this may seem, giving yourself rewards each time that you take a small, medium, or large step toward your publishing goals will do more to move you farther, and faster, down the road than anything else. This will happen because you will be immediately and consistently reversing the once errant thinking that caused you to believe that writing would be painful. So, remember to utilize the above lists each day as you begin on your route, and you will not only see your entire attitude toward the experience change dramatically but the fruits of your efforts will grow out of control as well.

Once you have made a promise to yourself to employ the above, you are done with this session.

*"No wind favors him who has not a destined port."*
Michel de Montaigne

# TEN

Now it's time to compose an ultimate, goal-affirming statement. Don't be shy when writing this statement. You can go back and change it at any time, but never do so in a time of fear or during a weak moment. It is not necessary for you to include a time limit to live this reality, but you can do so if you like.

Remember to relax and return to your special place, then allow your statement to be released through you. Take your time on the composition of this statement. It is by far the most important document that you will have written up to this point. Several sessions with yourself may be necessary. Use the statement daily, rewarding yourself appropriately for doing so. Because it covers and combines many additional areas not involved before, this statement should be much lengthier than the attitude-adjusting sentences we have been composing up to this point.

Take a look at the example that follows, then put together your own statement.

*"The 'What should be' never did exist, but people keep trying to live up to it. There is no 'What should be,' there is only what is."*

Lenny Bruce

*I have been placed on this earth to create and live my dreams. Up to this point, only my own misunderstandings have kept me from doing so. But right here and now, I confirm that I will do whatever is necessary to remove the blockages I have innocently placed before myself. I believe in myself, and I believe in my dream to widely influence the people of the world with my writing. As well, I believe in my destiny to live it.*

*Most importantly, I realize that no dream, or the hope for such, can long endure, unless built upon truth and goodness. Thus, I will embark on no action, or enter into any association, that will not benefit all parties concerned.*

*In addition, I will eliminate the derivatives of all my innocent misunderstandings, all envy, jealousy, hatred, selfishness, to make room for the living of my dream and all the good which is associated with it.*

*To this aim, I here and now promise to persistently and consistently devote myself.*

*My best,*

*Tom Bird*

# Eleven

If you have gone through all of the necessary exercises above, you are now ready to move on to the three steps for getting your work into print. Congratulations.

If you have skipped any of the aforementioned steps, go back and fully complete them before moving on. This is only being suggested with your best interests in mind.

---

*"We are not interested in the possibilities of defeat."*
*Queen Victoria*

# Step Two: Understanding Your Publishing Options

**2**

**GOAL: AVOIDING A WRITER'S SECOND BIGGEST MISTAKE BY CHOOSING THE APPROPRIATE OPTION FOR BOTH YOU AND YOUR PROJECT.**

# INTRODUCTION

By its literal, simple definition, publishing translates to the preparing and then issuing of material for distribution and/or sale to the public.

However, to most authors it equates to much, much more. It represents recognition leading to personal and professional advancement, the expression of talent, passion and intelligence, respect, and to the penning of a record destined to live on through the ages.

As a result, there is nothing more influential in our culture than the written, and especially, published word. It is the foundation for everything we have been taught and entertained by. As a result, no art form – not acting, sculpting, or painting – draws more respect than writing. Is it any wonder then that 81% of Americans, in a survey recently quoted by *The New York Times,* said that they felt they had a book inside of them?

*"He mobilized the English language and sent it into battle...."*
John Fitzgerald Kennedy

> "A good book is the best of friends, the same today and forever."
> — Martin

Yet, because of all the esteem lauded upon publishing and because those that teach it often have been so unsuccessful in approaching it themselves, an aura of impossibility has been draped around it.

I fully realize that there is a part of you, a self-sabotaging side, which is calling out for you to skip this section and instead launch yourself right into the nuts and bolts of getting published. But to do so would amount to literary suicide. The second biggest mistake that new writers make springs directly from not properly understanding their publishing options.

So, if getting published is sincerely your goal, read on.

# Chapter Two: Your Options

## Conventional Presses

As mentioned in the Introduction to this step, the sole purpose of publishing is to distribute and/or sell a form of your writing to the public. It is the conventional form of publishing, the first option we will examine, that we associate with the successful completion of this task. The conventional publishers no doubt do perform this task, but at what price to you, your career as an author, and to the potential of your work?

*"You never expected justice from a company, did you? They have neither a soul to lose nor a body to kick."*

Sydney Smith

# What a Book Publisher Is Supposedly Thought to Do

Let's first define what it is that most believe these houses are responsible for doing. As I will show, they are not the all-knowing, all-caring, soon-to-make-you-successful publishing option that you may believe them to be.

### Publish Your Book

The fact that they publish your book making it available to the public is absolutely correct.

### Manage Your Cash Flow

A publisher is responsible for collecting all monies, accounting for it, and passing off your share of the profits to you.

### Edit Your Book

The stories abound about how legendary authors stumbled upon just the right editor, and it was that one editor who ended up being the primary driving force behind the success in that writer's career.

If you believe that option is still available to you, think again. The book publishing industry no longer has the monopoly on America's entertainment time that it once did. As a result, over the past few decades conventional publishing houses have resorted to publishing hundreds of times more books at a smaller profit margin just

*"The big print giveth and the fine print taketh away."*
— J. Fulton Sheen

to keep up with cable, satellite television, videos, and other more convenient alternatives. The more books that a house is responsible for publishing, the more work that falls upon the shoulders of its editorial staff. However, most houses, in an attempt to keep down their overhead, have not increased the sizes of their editorial staffs to compensate for this shift. As a result, editors don't have the time they once had to transform you into a star.

In fact, it is you, as the author, who is responsible for making sure that your work has been edited before it is submitted.

## DISTRIBUTE YOUR BOOK

Conventional houses are indeed responsible for the distribution of your book. How well they complete this task, though, is up in the air. Will they simply hand it over to a nationally known distributor, will they utilize their own sales force as well, or in the best-case scenario, do both?

It is very important to have a crystal clear understanding about the depth of commitment of a conventional house before signing on.

## MARKET YOUR BOOK

Before we move on further into this topic, let me make it clear that marketing does not make a book into a bestseller. In fact, many a publisher has spent hundreds of thousands of dollars on a chosen book only to see the work land nowhere near a bestseller list.

Again, marketing does not make a book into a bestseller. It simply brings to the attention of a

*"Gentlemen, you must not mistake me. I admit that he is the sworn foe of our nation, and, if you will, of the whole human race. But gentlemen, we must be just to our enemy. We must not forget that he once shot a bookseller."*

Thomas Campbell

> *"The idea of going to a writers' congress in Moscow is rather like attending a human rights conference in Nazi Germany."*
> — David Markstein

certain influential audience the release of the book. From that time forward, the book must stand on its own. It is word-of-mouth which is truly responsible for turning a book into a bestseller.

The vast majority of conventional publishers rely on an author to do his or her own marketing. To fool yourself into believing that once you sign on with a conventional publisher that your house will promotionally take care of everything is delusional.

Even if a conventional publisher does decide to get involved with the promotion of your book, there is a more than excellent chance that their tiny marketing and publicity staff can't handle the workload. Conventional publishing houses are also notoriously poor payers. Thus they don't attract the finest promotional minds. So, even if they tried to promote your book, they probably could not follow through in a competent manner.

In fact, the marketing abilities of a conventional publisher are oftentimes so inadequate that even if a house does decide to promote an author's book, in most cases they have to employ the services of an outside firm to do it for them.

## DESIGN THE ARTWORK FOR YOUR BOOK

Conventional publishers absorb the responsibility of the artwork associated with your book. But keep in mind that you will be using their artists and, thus, you may not have as much artistic control over how your product looks as you would like.

## COPYRIGHT YOUR BOOK

Conventional publishers will copyright your book in your name and take the responsibility for performing other small legal tasks, including procuring the ISBN number. However, they will not take responsibility for offering you any sort of legal protection. In fact, as part of your contract, they will make you sign a waiver making themselves immune from any problems you may run into.

## REPRESENT THE SPECIALTY RIGHTS FOR YOUR BOOK TO OTHER PUBLISHING OPTIONS

Part of a conventional publisher's role is to serve as a clearinghouse for the rights of your book. For example, a conventional publisher may purchase the hardback rights for your book. But the house may also serve as the agent to market your paperback rights to another house, as well as your serial rights, the reprinting of excerpts from your book in magazines and newspapers, and book club rights. For their role in any transaction of this sort, they normally expect to receive 50% of all revenues generated.

## LITERARY AGENT NEEDED

Even though it is not an absolute must in each and every case, the vast majority of all conventional publishers, including all the top houses, refuse to review any material written by a new writer who is not represented by a literary agent. This rule is in place to safeguard against

*"He is the only man who is forever apologizing for his occupation."*

H. L. Mencken

a waste of time on their end by ensuring that you have the credibility necessary to justify their time for a review. More on this is covered later. An agent's total take is normally 15% of your gross revenue, plus reimbursement of all his or her out-of-pocket expenses.

> *"Publish and be damned."*
> Duke of Wellington

## THE ADVANCE

Initially, if a conventional publisher is relatively interested in your work, you will be offered an advance. An advance is defined as "risk money applied against potential royalties earned."

Here's how it works. Let's say that you accept a $10,000 advance from a publisher, your book eventually sells for $20, and your 10% royalty rate is based on the cover price of the book. It can also be based on the net return received by the publisher. But, in that case, you would normally receive a much higher royalty rate to compensate for the discount afforded a bookstore or distributor. As it is, royalty rates range between 5-25%. However, in the case above where your royalty rate was based on the cover price, you would receive $2 per book sold. In that case, then, how many books would your book need to sell to make back the advance you were offered? Correct: 5,000.

What would happen if your book sold only 3,000 copies? Would you then be responsible for returning $4,000? Legally, you would be liable for the return of the unearned portion of the advance. However, if you have fulfilled your obligations as outlined under your contract with the publisher, rarely would you be expected to repay any part of your advance.

## THE AMOUNT OF MONEY YOU ACTUALLY RECEIVE

Let's use the scenario from above to sketch out how much money you would actually receive from the sale of your book.

For example, if your book sells the lofty total of 60,000 books. You would receive $120,000, minus your agent's commission of 15%, for a total of $102,000. This, of course, does not include the monies generated by your publisher for outside sales to book clubs, paperback rights, etc., of which your house would receive a minimum of 50%.

How much is then pocketed by your publisher? In the case where your house sold 60,000 of your books on a straight 40% discount rate to stores that would mean that their gross revenue per book would end up being $12. However, after their production costs of $3 and the $2 they would have to pay you were subtracted, they would end up clearing $7 per book, or two or three times as much money as you were awarded for doing the bulk of the work by writing the book.

## THE 90-10 REALITY

Please keep in mind that, especially in today's world, the vast majority of publishing houses are owned by Fortune 500 companies who care about nothing other than the bottom line. Thus, in essence, conventional publishers are nothing more or less than venture capitalists. Thus, they are willing to absorb a high risk on each of their dollars invested in exchange for a potential high return.

---

**Amount You Receive**

| | |
|---|---:|
| Books Sold | 60,000 |
| Royalty | x $2 |
| | 120,000 |
| Agent's 15% | - 18,000 |
| Total | $102,000 |

**Amount Your Publisher Receives**

| | |
|---|---:|
| Gross per Book | $12 |
| Production | - $3 |
| Royalty | - $2 |
| Net per Book | $7 |
| Books Sold (40% dis.) | 60,000 |
| | x $7 |
| | $420,000 |

---

"Whenever ideas fail, men invent words."
　　　　　Martin H. Fischer

> "The business of America is business."
> —Calvin Coolidge

They are in the business to make money — period. They are not interested in influencing society or nurturing the career of a bright new writer, unless doing so would offer them a high return on their investment dollar.

How much bottom line revenue you and your book are worth, then, is their only consideration. What you and your book can generate for them is how they look at you. One of the ways that you can become more attractive to them is directly tied to what you will do to market your own book.

Yes, if you were under the misimpression that today's conventional publishers actually follow through on all of the tasks listed above, think again. Unless you fall into the good fortune of being one of their top 10% advances, do not expect them to put out any monies for the editorial work that might be needed on your book or for marketing it. You will be expected to deliver your manuscript to them in nearly perfect form. Plus, you will be responsible for doing all of the necessary promotion work and for paying for any advertisements, publicity, or for signing talk show tours.

So important is your willingness to directly contribute in this area that a conventional publisher will actually expect you to state up front, before your book is considered for publication, how much you will be willing to offer marketing-wise toward the promotion of your own work. By limiting the monies they are expected to kick in, they severely limit their liability. As a result, instantly, the $2 per book you could earn looks really small. This is especially the case if you decide to follow through on their suggestion to hire a professional publicity/marketing firm to promote your book. The rates for any of these firms usually range from $32,000-$45,000.

So, for example, if you grossed the $102,000 via your 60,000-book sale stated earlier, and had to spend $40,000 promotionally, you would then have earned only $62,000, while your conventional publisher would have taken in $420,000 — exactly the type of return a venture capitalist would expect.

Poverty is oftentimes associated with writing, but it is not because money is not being generated. It is only because so little of it is offered to the author, who has been standing for this type of misaligned business deal for centuries.

## CREDIBILITY

Conventional publishers may rob you of your artistic, editorial, and literary freedom. They may offer you an insultingly low share of the profits, but a big-name, conventional publisher who lends you their good name offers you what no one else can — credibility. And it is credibility that most educated readers, who are also the best book buyers, relate to.

As a result of this credibility, more doors will be opened for you and your book personally, professionally, and literarily. The same credibility sets the foundation for sales. But unfortunately, if you do not receive monies from a publisher to make you one of their top 10% properties, they won't promote your work.

Without promotion, the credibility is just that — credibility. However, no matter how applauded it is, without the necessary exposure of promotion, there is a superior chance that it

| Amount You Receive | |
|---|---|
| Books Sold | 60,000 |
| Royalty | x $2 |
| | 120,000 |
| Agent's 15% | - 18,000 |
| Total | $102,000 |
| Promotion | - $ 40,000 |
| | $ 62,000 |

*"It's like having a license to print your own money."*
Lord Thomson of Fleet

will not translate into sales. And, if your book doesn't sell well, all credibility will be lost. So, it becomes a roll of the dice if you choose to go the conventional route.

> "Literature is the art of writing something that will be read twice."
> Cyril Connolly

# SELF-PUBLICATION

## FORMER DRAWBACKS OF SELF-PUBLISHING

Neale Donald Walsch, who wrote the country's bestselling *Conversations with God* series; literary legends Mark Twain, James Joyce, D. H. Lawrence, Stephen Crane, Edgar Allen Poe, Rudyard Kipling, Walt Whitman, George Bernard Shaw, Ezra Pound, Henry David Thoreau, Zane Gray, Carl Sandburg, and present-day literary legends John Grisham and James Redfield of the *Celestine Prophecy* connection, what two aspects do they all have in common?

First, their initial works all fell outside the lines of the ordinary, making them trendsetters. As a result, and secondly, they were left no alternative than to prove their worth by self-publishing.

Self-publishing is not the dregs to which the failed writer is left to retreat. Quite the contrary, it is the path of initiation for those trendsetters who oftentimes – like those mentioned above – go on to influence us the most. The publishing industry, being a hotbed of venture capitalists, is always and only looking for the safe and sure bet. Because their brilliance falls outside the ranks of the norm, trendsetters simply do not fit through the very narrow doorway of the conventional house.

Up until the last few years, though, no matter how popular an alternative it might have been for the trendsetter, self-publishing was littered with drawbacks.

## EXPENSIVE

Until recently, the cost to produce a book was normally outside what an average American could spare or would want to spend. Just to have a manuscript typeset would often cost tens of thousands of dollars. Add into that the cost of a qualified style editor and you easily are in the $30,000 range. Then, in the past, to bring down the cost-per-unit price of one's book, high quantity first runs of 10,000 copies or more were a necessity. So, the author would have no choice other than to sink at least another $40,000 into inventory, bringing his initial cash outlay to around $70,000.

## LESS THAN WORTHY ALTERNATIVES

As the result of, and because of an author's general lack of understanding and desperation, the door was oftentimes left wide open for the seemingly attractive vanity or subsidy presses to wield their evil wands. Their claims stated that they could supposedly do all that needed to be done better and at a price much lower than doing it on one's own. However, these presses, long the poisons of academics and vulnerable senior citizens, received the poor reputation they have for a reason.

*"Only two classes of books are of universal appeal. The very best and the very worst."*
Ford Maddox Ford

Yes, they produced books, but these works were often poorly edited, poorly designed, and rarely ever promoted. As well, normally only enough copies were printed to soothe the author's fledgling ego. All of this was done, of course, so that the vanity or subsidy houses could keep as much of the fee charged to the author as possible. Sure, authors were often allowed as much as a 75% royalty rate, which was so attractive that their eyes bulged. However, no matter how you look at it, 75% of nothing is still nothing.

The extraordinary royalty rate was like the scent of blood to a hungry shark. Once the hopeful author was reeled in, the vanity or subsidy publisher would simply focus on getting the job done quickly and cheaply so as to keep as much of the fee charged to the writer as possible. To the vanity or subsidy house, promotion is too much work and the potential profit earned too slight to be considered even remotely attractive — especially when the next hungry sucker with the wide-open checkbook is usually waiting eagerly around the bend.

## Distribution

Even if one did self-publish, and somehow ended up with a saleable product, getting it in bookstores and distributed across the country was a whole new problem. In most cases, though, the future of a worthy book died on the dusty shelves in the author's garage or attic.

*"Literature flourishes best when it is half a trade and half an art."*

Dean Inge

## THE SELF-PUBLISHING SOLUTION

Though it may only have been by the sheer quality of their works and the Divine Guidance associated with them, the authors mentioned at the beginning of this section actually made it. However, the Divine, in today's market, has offered up a larger amount of assistance for those who choose to self-publish. That solution is referred to as *Print On Demand presses* or *POD publishing*.

As a result of the advent of the computer age, much has changed in the publishing industry in the last few years. The cost of typesetting a book, now commonly referred to as formatting, has dropped from tens of thousands of dollars to around the $1500 range. The computer age has also enabled books to be stored in the memory of a computer and to be called forward at any time – the best time being when someone is ready and willing to purchase it. Thus evolved the name for this type of publishing alternative. Because of the computer age, a book can literally be called forward from memory and generated at the request of a buyer or potential purchaser. As a result, no major inventory has to be purchased by the author, eliminating costly expense number two, and the cost to publish a book dropped from $70,000 to around the $2,000-$3,000 range.

Most POD presses also offer you a turn-around time (from receiving your manuscript and transforming it into a fully published book) of less than 30 days. Conventional presses take on average of between 9-13 months to perform the same task.

Add to that the fact that the most influential distributor of books in the world, Ingram,

*"Literature is mostly about having sex and not much about having children; life is the other way around."*
David Lodge

through its offshoot Lightning Source, has spearheaded this jolt to the industry, by opening its own POD press. (www.lightningsource.com for more information) So, Lightning Source will place your formatted book on their computer system, print however many copies are necessary, and send them out whenever there is an order. They will also collect the money paid for your book(s) and send it to you, and they offer international distribution as well. In fact, when you sign up with Lightning Source, there is practically nowhere of affluence on the planet that your book will not be available for purchase. So, Lightning Source will offer you many of the essential luxuries of a conventional press without having to give up 85-90% of your profit.

*"The reading of all good books is like a conversation with the finest men of past centuries."*
— Rene Descartes

## WHAT A POD PRESS DOES OFFER

Just to keep straight all the information you have been exposed to so far, a legitimate POD press, such as Lightning Source, collects the money from purchases of your book and passes it along to you. So, they manage your cash flow. They also store your manuscript in their computer, print and publish it at a 'per book' price to you, and distribute it, making it available to individuals and bookstores all across the globe.

## WHAT A POD PRESS DOES NOT OFFER

In essence, with a worthy POD house you will be serving as your own publisher. So, you will need to form a specific business entity to do so and give it a name. This can normally be accomplished for between $10-$100, depending upon in which state you live.

As a result of accepting the reins of being your own publisher, the POD press is left being what it is and is only – a printing house with distributing capabilities. This, of course, is what self-publishing houses, such as vanity or subsidy presses, have always been. However, in the past, these cagey creatures have been able to pass themselves off as more and thus, wound up charging more than they were worth. Thus the POD route is not only fast, efficient, and inexpensive, but is the most honest and forthright business deal yet offered the literary author/entrepreneur.

Again, what the POD press **does** do is print, distribute your book, and manage your cash flow for you. These services come at the cost of a modest, up-front fee of approximately $400 and the price it costs to print your book, which is in the range of $4 per paperback book and $8 for hardcover. This price is approximately 25% higher per book than you would expect to pay if you employed the past form of self-publishing. This is where a POD house makes its profit. However, if you go the POD route, you will also avoid the purchase and cost of carrying a big inventory.

What the POD house **does not do** is edit your book, take responsibility for the artwork, promote your book to other houses for the sale of other rights, or sell directly to the public. That is left up to you. But, again, outside the design of your work, conventional publishers would expect you to take care of all the editorial content and promote it as well. Also, you would hand over to them between 85-90% of your profit, while with a POD house you keep 100% of the gross.

---

## YOUR OPTIONS

**What They Do and Don't Do For You**

**Conventional Publisher**
*(for the 'not in top 10%')*

- *Publish Your Book*
- *Manage Your Cash Flow*
- *Little or No Editing*
- *Offer Wide Distribution*
- *Little or No Marketing*
- *Artwork Designed by Staff (little or no input from you)*
- *Procure Copyright/ISBN*
- *Limited Legal Protection*
- *Represent Specialty Rights*
- *Require Literary Agent*
- *Offer Advance of Royalties*
- *Offer Reader Credibility*
- *Keep 85-90% of Profits*

**Print on Demand Presses**

- *You Pay to Publish the Book*
- *Manage Your Cash Flow*
- *Offers Wide Distribution*
- *You Control Marketing*
- *You Hire an Editor*
- *You Choose the Book Designer and Layout*
- *Art Designed by Your Artist*
- *You Obtain Copyright/ISBN*
- *You Manage Specialty Rights*
- *No Literary Agent Necessary*
- *No Advance of Royalties*
- *No Credibility*
- *You Retain 100% of Profit*

## WHAT DOES IT COST TO GO POD?

The following options vary greatly in cost. In reality, you can self-publish your POD book for as little as $500 if you choose to do the vast majority of the labor yourself.

I had one student go this route with her novel. However, despite the depth of her idea, her drive, and her passionate prose, the book looked like she had handled all of the tasks herself, and its dire need for editing took much away from the eventual success of the story. So, I wouldn't recommend going this route. Even though this student was able to clear her bottom line quickly, I strongly feel that her work lived a life far less than its potential. However, what you choose to do with the following is completely up to you. Just make sure you can live with your choices while offering your literary baby the chance it deserves.

### FORMATTING

Formatting translates to converting your manuscript into the design of a book. The person you hire for this task is by far the most important individual you will deal with. No matter how much work you put into your book, if you try to skimp here to save a few bucks, and the formatter you hire does a less-than-adequate job, your book will look terrible. As a result, your book sales will wane, if not disappear altogether.

Make sure as well that your formatter has worked with the POD press you choose. If he or

*"The proper study of mankind is books."*
  Aldous Huxley

she has not, you may wind up paying for this person's education to learn how to do so.

Ask to see examples of this person's work, and don't be shy to request a list of professional references. Let your potential formatters read some of your manuscript before signing on. Not only will this give you an idea of how sincere the person is, but doing so will also allow you to audit and compare any ideas they may have for formatting your book. This person needs to be not only technically sound and proven, but creative and artistic as well.

Good formatters are hard to find, so start searching for this person as soon as possible.

To find competent formatters, you can check out my website, www.ambassu.com, or contact the POD press which you are most interested in, or call printers in your area for recommendations. Some PODs will even provide this service for you. Get potential formatters to quote you a flat fee, which is the best way to prevent any hidden costs and foul-ups on their end that could end up costing you more than you planned. Depending upon the length of your book and the style in which you will want it formatted, this option would cost you between $600-$1800. If that sounds like a lot of money to you, please keep in mind how important the presentation of your book is, as well as the fact that only a few years ago this service, via typesetting, would have cost you tens of thousands of dollars.

## COVER DESIGN

Again, like the student mentioned previously, you can do this yourself. However, there is a

*"A business that makes nothing but money is a poor kind of business."*

Henry Ford

good chance that your potential readers will be able to tell. In that case, you may lose book sales. The first thing that a potential reader sees is the cover of your book. If it looks unprofessional or does not grab his or her attention, you lose a sale.

As with formatters, a good cover artist is hard to find. A cover artist needs to be creative, so don't be afraid to ask for a review of their ideas on your book cover before entering into any type of agreement. Ask for professional references and examples of previous covers. Make sure, too, that he or she is intimately familiar with meeting the demands of your POD house. Otherwise, you may end up paying for the education this person should already possess.

Avoid, at all costs, web services whose prices seem cheaper than others but offer only a few stock styles of cover for you to choose from. It is best and most professional looking if you have something individually created for your cover.

As with formatters, start looking for this person early and get candidates to quote you a flat rate. Average costs for this service range from $600-$900. Potential recommendations for cover artists can be found from the same sources as formatters.

## Editing

Even if you were one of those few young adults or children who somehow picked up the force-feeding of grammar, punctuation, and spelling while in school, at some point you will become blind to a credible review of your own work. So, it is essential that you have your book copyedited by someone else – hopefully a profes-

*"Great Literature is simply language charged with meaning to the utmost possible degree."*
Ezra Pound

sional – before handing it over to your formatter.

The *Literary Market Place* (LMP), which is available in any good library, is highly recommended as a source for copyeditors. A reasonable cost for copyediting a book is $2.00 per page.

There is also a second type and potentially more important brand of this work that needs to be taken into consideration as well, and that is style editing.

You need to have your book style edited if you just have not done everything necessary to properly compose your work. To avoid this potentially large and unnecessary expense, I strongly suggest applying the step-by-step method shared in my book *Your Artist Within*.

However, if you already have a manuscript fully completed or if after employing the methods in *Your Artist Within* you still feel you need the services of a style editor, listings of sources can be found in the *Literary Market Place* (LMP – available in all libraries) or on my website.

Make sure when interviewing potential candidates for this position that you request the usual references and examples of work. Let your candidates also review a sampling of your work to see what suggestions they may have for improvement.

As you go over your candidates' suggestions for improvement, pay very special attention to their objectivity. You want to ensure that you will be working with an objective editor and not a frustrated writer. In the case of the latter, this person will attempt to rewrite your book for you in their style, as opposed to trying to aid you in bringing out your own voice. Prices for a competent style editor range from $2500-$10,000.

*"Was there ever yet anything written by mere man that was wished longer by its readers."*

Samuel Johnson,
excerpting from *Don Quixote, Robinson Crusoe, and The Pilgrim's Progress*

> "Publication is the male equivalent of childbirth."
> Richard Acland

## Legal

As mentioned, you will need to form your own business entity to go the POD route, which can range anywhere in cost from $10-$100. I would also suggest that you at least run your chosen arrangement by a competent accountant or attorney. I routinely budget $250, which is normally more than enough to cover the cost of the review.

One way or another, you will also be responsible for the copyrighting of your material. When choosing your POD house, check into what services they offer. Do they handle the copyright of your material or do you?

If you are responsible for your own, you can complete the task online for approximately $30 through the Library of Congress. Your attorney can also handle it as well. With an attorney's fee included, it would cost several hundred dollars more than the $30 charged if you go directly through the Library of Congress.

If you would like an attorney to review your manuscript for any potential legally dangerous statements or claims, a service normally provided by conventional houses, there are plenty of lawyers qualified to do so. They can be found under the title of Intellectual Property Attorneys.

However, when you boil it all down, all that is legally necessary for you to do is start your own company. As mentioned, the costs for this service run between $10-$100, but it is suggested that you budget $250 just in case you choose to seek the advice of a professional. Thus, unless you decide it's worth the thousands of dollars it would take to obtain an attorney to review your manuscript, I suggest that budgeting $250 would be more than sufficient.

## PROMOTION

Once, at an Intensive Retreat I was offering in my home in Sedona, Arizona, Dick O'Connor, a longtime, New York editor I had brought in to copresent, made a very interesting point.

In trying to illustrate where it was that our students should focus their promotional attention as authors, he drew a small dot in the middle of a flip chart.

"What is this?" he asked.

After no one replied, Dick answered for them. "The number of Americans who read hardback books."

Then he drew a small circle around the dot and asked, "What's this?"

Again, no one dared to answer, so he replied for them a second time. "The number of people who read paperback books."

Then Dick drew a huge circle around the smaller circle, and asked for a third time, "What's this?"

No longer waiting for a response, Dick replied quickly this time to his own query. "Those who don't read books."

The point I'm trying to make here is that expensive major media blanket advertising is a waste of time for authors. There is a small, enthusiastic audience that needs to be approached. After that has been successfully completed, you can just do as any other publisher would do, rely on word of mouth to sell your book for you.

If you are writing fiction, the best way to do this is through reviews written on your book. The three most influential reviewers in the industry, because they cater mostly to the large-scale pur-

*"The ratio of literacy to illiteracy is constant, but nowadays the illiterates can read and write."*
Alberto Moravia

> *"No furniture is so charming as books."*
>
> Sydney Smith

chasers of books, are *Publishers Weekly*, *Kirkus Reviews*, and *The Library Journal*. Each of these publications has sites on the Internet that will tell you exactly what needs to be done to have your book considered for a review. Keep in mind, though, that with these three reviewers, or any others, it is in your best interest to get your book, even if it is in rough form, into their hands as far in advance of your planned publication date as possible.

As far as other magazines, syndication services, and newspapers are concerned, the corporate names and addresses can be found in the *Literary Market Place* (LMP) and *Publishers and Editors Yearbook*, both of which are usually available at libraries.

As far as costs for promoting your fiction is concerned, all you need to do is set aside enough cash to cover the expenses of review copies and their mailing costs. Besides that, all you will need is a website.

Now, I know that it is possible to set up a website for under $50. The trouble with that site, though, is that it looks like a website that you set up for under $50. Because so much of the world is cyber-attuned it is important to have a nice site.

Scan the Internet for the websites of some of your favorite authors and take notes of what they have done. Then use either an Internet service or personal references to help you access lists of site designers. Follow the same procedures that you employed when acquiring the services of your editor, artist, or formatter. Ask for references and for them to offer you ideas on what they would do with your site. Ask for examples of their work as well. Accept only a flat, all-inclusive price as their bid to enable you to avoid the mystery and disappointment of the hourly rate. Also, make sure your webmaster has the abilities to upload your materials on your book to major bookselling sites such as Amazon.com and BarnesandNoble.com, and to attune your website to the liking of search engines, which will eventually lead to your popularity on the Internet.

Including the reservation of your website name, yearly fees, and your programmer's labor, I would budget $1200.

Regarding non-fiction, beyond the use of reviews and a well-done website to stimulate interest in your book, radio and television interviews are also a large asset. The finest route to gain access to every TV and radio interviewer in the country is through a publication titled *Radio-Television Interview Reporter* (RTIR).

RTIR sports listings and descriptions of books and their authors and is sent out three times a month to every major and minor media source in the country. Over 21,000 media are contacted with each mailing.

RTIR usually offers a collection of specials all ranging in the area of $1200 per six-ad contract, which covers not only the running of six of your ads, but an array of other services and products as well, including a database of their entire media mailing list.

I highly recommend the use of this service. Like most good businesses, RTIR has an extensive website which can answer all of your questions.

Lastly, to best understand all of the promotional opportunities available to you, I strongly suggest your reading Rick Frishman's books

*"If you pay peanuts, you get monkeys."*
James Goldsmith

*Guerrilla Marketing* and *Guerrilla Publicity for Writers*.

Rick is the president of the largest and most influential book publicity firm in the world, Planned Television Arts (or PTA), and he is a marketing genius. Even though each of his two books costs only $14.95, they are worth their weight in gold.

Read both books, take notes if you like, and then start playing with the valuable suggestions Rick makes. Choose what feels comfortable to you, leave the rest behind, and then just keep promoting.

PTA also works out a special deal for my students as long as you are willing to do the majority of the legwork. If you would like their direct assistance in promoting your book, they will design a professional promotional campaign for you and implement it over half a year for $1500 per month. Even though this may sound expensive, the services and instructions you will receive are comparable to what some conventional publishers pay 3-4 times as much for. The big difference is that you wind up doing the majority of the legwork, but the price is a very good investment, especially if a full-time author is what you want to be.

## CREDIBILITY

While a conventional publisher oftentimes offers credibility, the POD press, especially since you will be publishing under the name of your own house, cannot help you in that area.

However, book sales equate to reputations and good reputations equate to credibility. So, the

> *"As repressed sadists are supposed to become policemen or butchers so those with irrational fear of life become publishers."*
> — Cyril Connolly

## POD Costs

You can tailor your POD publishing plan to your taste and budget. However, to make your decision easier for you, I decided to plot the two extremes for you. Like most of my students, you will probably end up spending a total somewhere in the middle.

| Low Budget | Expenditures | High Budget |
|---|---|---|
| – | Formatting | $1,500 |
| $ 450 | Cover Design | $ 900 |
| – | Copyediting (based on a 300-page book) | $ 600 |
| – | Style Editing | $2,500 |
| $ 250 | Legal | $ 250 |
| $2,000 | Promotion Review Copies (250 copies @ $5 each plus $3 each mailing) | $2,000 |
| – | RTIR ad | $1,200 |
| $ 600 | POD Publisher | $ 600 |
|  | Addition of Professional Publicist | $9,000 |
| $3,300 | TOTALS | $18,550 |

> *"Thanks to words, we have been able to rise above the brutes; and thanks to words, we have often sunk to the level of demons."*
>
> — Aldous Huxley

better job you do, the more book sales you will gain, and the more credibility you will be building for your house.

Hardly anyone had heard of tiny Hampton Roads Press until they published Walsh's *Conversations with God*, which they eventually sold to Putnam who made it into a bestseller. Now, everyone in the publishing world knows of Hampton Roads as one of the finest New Age publishers in the business. All it takes is one big book.

## Choosing the Right POD House

Even though the POD industry is relatively new, it hasn't taken long for some unworthy alternatives to infiltrate the most innovative, author-friendly step forward in the history of publishing. But since there is no inner governing body of ethics in this industry, which keeps snakes from creeping in, it is up to you, the author and the most important spoke in the publishing wheel, to discern for yourself who is right and wrong for you.

Your decision should boil down to a few basic facts:

1. <u>Turnaround Time</u>: How quickly will the POD house be able to produce your book? Don't settle for anything over 30 working days.

2. <u>Background</u>: Ask for references and samples of books they have published. Time in business is also an important factor.

3. <u>Cost</u>:  How much do they charge and especially what is it that you can expect for your fee?

4. <u>Print Cost</u>:  How much will it cost to have your book printed, and how quickly can they promise to get orders out for you?

5. <u>Royalties</u>:  A true POD house doesn't pay royalties to their authors because the authors are given 100% of all monies received. Now, there are those houses who refer to themselves as PODs who proudly proclaim they pay their authors a whopping 25% royalty rate. Let me straighten this out for you. You pay for all the expenses to have your book edited and printed, and they don't provide any type of service at all in these cases. You write the book and then you pay them to simply add it to their computer database. Then they profit from every book you have printed and they want to receive 75% of the monies from the sale of the book? For doing what? May those with eyes actually see the truth behind such a scandal. In fact, may even those without eyes see it.

6. <u>Credibility</u>:  At this juncture in their development, a POD press does not offer you any credibility. If someone from a POD house tells you that your association with their name does offer you credibility – run, don't walk, away from them.

> "Grasshopper, look beyond the game, as you look beneath the surface of the pool to see its depth."
> Master Po, *"Kung Fu"*

## Distribution

Ingram is the finest, most accepted, and best known distributor of books in the world. If a POD house that you are considering does not use them, you should ask why. No other distributor of books even comes close to matching up.

What I suggest doing is rating each POD press in each of the categories listed above from 1-10 with 10 being the highest rating. Then, since the topic of royalties and distribution are the two most important categories for the long-term, double whatever the score each POD alternative comes up with in those two areas. Then add up your totals and the highest score should be the right POD house for you.

# Articles, Short Stories, and Poetry

Contrary to what you may have been told, articles, short stories, and poetry are not the best door to go through to become the published author of books you may want to be. In fact, quite the opposite is true. If you want to write articles, short stories, and poetry, the most successful way to do so is to first become a known commodity as a successful author of books.

Even though I have included in this book information on this alternative, I simply do not recommend it as a quick, painless, and direct route to authoring books.

*"A classic-something that everybody wants to have read and nobody wants to read."*
Mark Twain

# The Ultimate of All Solutions

Let's keep in mind that whatever it is that you have coming through to write, or which has already come through you and has been written, is like your literary child, and as with a child of any sort, you want the best for it. How you offer this child to the public is where publishing comes in.

Forget about all the prestige, wealth, and fame that you may have inappropriately associated with publishing. All publishing is really there to do is to make available to the public whatever literary gift you may have. That's it.

When looking at it from that perspective, choosing the right publishing option is really not much different than picking the right college or university to further a child's education and training.

Beyond all the financial drawbacks and the loss of artistic, editorial, and literary control, the conventional publishers, because of the credibility associated with them and the massive influence and money they can put behind you if you end up being in their top 10% books, are still the best option. Thus I suggest that you wholeheartedly pursue that option first. How to do just that is what the majority of the remainder of this book is devoted to showing you.

After you have played out that option and if you do not land a contract as one of a publisher's top 10% books, then go the POD route, which will teach you more about the world of publishing than you ever thought possible.

*"My motto is to be published and be sued."*
　　　　　　　　　Richard Ingrams

Once you've used POD to sell a few thousand copies of your book, proving that there is indeed a market for it, reapproach the world of conventional publishing if you like, or stay with POD if you like. Either way, your valuable literary child will have found its way into the world – which is simply what publishing is there to provide and nothing more.

# CHECKLIST

To help you understand what needs to be performed and when, I have included a slightly modified checklist as designed by one of my students, Shirley Hildreth of Muse Imagery in Las Vegas, Nevada. Shirley has become so successful at organizing this system that she has now begun working with new authors in leading them through this process.

At the conclusion of Shirley's checklist, I have also included some sample announcements and review response forms also utilized by Shirley.

*"If a book is worth reading, it is worth buying."*
                    John Ruskin

# THE SPIRIT OF PUBLISHING | Publishing Checklist

**STEP ONE, YOUR BUSINESS FOUNDATION:**

Form a Corporation

Acquire an Employer Identification Number

Acquire a Sales Tax/State Business License

Acquire City Business License

Acquire a Lightning Source Account


**STEP TWO, YOUR BOOK:**

Write Book

Choose Size

Decide on Price

Choose Cover Designer

Choose Text Formatter for Layout and Design

Choose Potential Text Editor

Choose Potential Style Editor

Put Together Illustrations, Gather Photographs

Write Extraneous Information:

    Author's Bio

    Acknowledgments

    Dedication

    Contact Page

    Order Page

    Teaser

Acquire Accolades/Endorsements

Get Permission Slips for Endorsements Signed

# THE SPIRIT OF PUBLISHING | Publishing Checklist

## STEP THREE, PROTECTING YOUR PRODUCT:

Consider Acquiring a Trademark

Acquire Trademark Verification from an Attorney

Acquire a Copyright – Library of Congress; Text: $30.00

Acquire a Copyright – Library of Congress; Cover: $30.00

Acquire a Copyright – LOC; published book: Form TX w/in 3 months of printing – 2 copies of book plus $30.00

Acquire Library of Congress – Pre-assigned control number (PCN); www.loc.gov

Acquire Library of Congress Cataloging in Publication Division (CIP); Send book. (You are only eligible to participate in the CIP program after you have published three books.)

Acquire Bowker International Standard Business Number (ISBN); www.bowkerlink.com

Acquire Bowker Registration; www.bowkerlink.com

## STEP FOUR, PROMOTION:

Construct a Media/News Kit

Collect Testimonials

Write Interview Questions

Write Press Release

Choose Excerpt from Book

Construct a Sample Flyer

Write a News/Press Release

Design Promotional Bookmarks as Handouts

Design a Business Card

Design Stationery

Design a Website

# THE SPIRIT OF PUBLISHING | Publishing Checklist

Join the Publishers Marketing Association; www.pma-online.org

Join the American Association of Publishers

Join the American Booksellers Association; www.bookweb.org

      ABA BookBuyer's Handbook; www.bookweb.com

List with the Contemporary Authors; www.galegroup.com

List in International Directory of Little Mag & Small Press; www.dustbooks.com

List in the Literary Marketplace; www.literarymarketplace.com

List in the Publishers Directory; www.galegroup.com

List in the Small Press Record of Books In Print (also International Dir.); www.dustbooks.com

List in Bowker Books In Print; www.bowkers.com

Enhance Listing on Amazon.com; www.amazon.com

Enhance Listing on Barnes & Noble; www.barnesandnoble.com

Enhance Listing on Books a Million; www.booksamillion.com

List on www.seekbooks.com

List on www.elgrande.com

**Reviews:**

Publishers Weekly; www.publishersweekly.com/abput/forecast-guidelines.asp

Library Journal; Send Galley or Book; www.libraryjournal.com/about/submission.asp

Kirkus Reviews; www.kirkusreviews.com

Booklist (American Library Association); www.ala.org

New York Times Book Review; www.nytimes.com/books

LA Times Book Review; www.latimes.com

Forward Magazine; www.forwardmagazine.com

Baker & Taylor; www.btol.com

Booklist (American Library Assoc.); www.ala.org/booklist

# THE SPIRIT OF PUBLISHING | Publishing Checklist

Chicago Tribune Books; www.chicagotribune.com/leisure/books

Ruminator Review; www.ruminator.com

H. W. Wilson Co.; www.hwwilson.com

Independent Publisher; www.bookpublishing.com

Ingram Book Group; www.ingrambookgroup.com

Kirkus Reviews; www.kirkusreviews.com

Library Journal; www.libraryjournal.com

Library of Congress Acquisitions; www.loc.gov

Library of Congress CIP; www.loc.gov

Los Angeles Times Book Review; www.latimes.com

Midwest Book Review; www.execpc.com/~mbr/bookwatch

Newsday; www.newsday.com

New York Review of Books; www.nybooks.com

New York Times (send out first); www.nytimes.com/books

Publishers Weekly; www.publishersweekly.com

Rainbo Electronic Reviews; www.rainboreviews.com

Reader's Digest Select Editions; www.readersdigest.com

San Francisco Chronicle; www.sfgate.com/eguide/books

Small Press Review; www.dustbooks.com

USA Today; www.usatoday.com

Voice Literary Supplement; www.villagevoice.com

Washington Post (send out first); www.washingtonpost.com

**Book Clubs:**

www.literarymarketplace.com

Book-of-the-Month Club; www.bookspan.com

# THE SPIRIT OF PUBLISHING | Publishing Checklist

Doubleday Select; www.booksonline.com

Literary Guild; www.literaryguild.com

Writer's Digest Book Club; www.writersdigest.com

**Other:**

Contact Radio/TV Talk Shows

Design Author Promotion Tour

Schedule Autograph Parties

Schedule Speaking Engagements

Schedule Book Fairs

Schedule Book Expo America (May); www.bookexpo.com

Potentially Schedule Frankfurt Book Fair (October); www.frankfurt-book-fair.com

# THE SPIRIT OF PUBLISHING | Publishing Checklist

## PRE-PUBLICATION REVIEW MAILING

Documents included in the Pre-Publication Review Mailing sent 4 to 5 months prior to publish date:

Cover letter
Bound Galley with Book Review Slip as cover (sample enclosed)
    News Release
Author Bio including a section listing Future Books By The Author
Fax Response Transmittal Sheet (sample enclosed – you may want to change the name, etc.)
SASE addressed to the publisher (the cover letter requested a clipping/tear sheet of the review)

## POST-PUBLICATION REVIEW MAILING

Documents included in the Post-Publication Review Mailing:

Cover letter
Published Book
Review Slip included as an informational 8.5 x 11 sheet (sample enclosed)
ABI Form copy
4" x 6" or larger, photo of book cover
Flyer/brochure
Testimonials
News Release
Author Bio
Expanded informational sheet explaining the question – What makes _____
  (name of book) unique?
Expanded informational sheet explaining – Who is the audience for _____
  (name of book)?
Fax Response Transmittal Sheet (sample enclosed – you may want to change the name, etc.)
SASE addressed to the publisher (the cover letter requested a clipping/tear sheet of the review)

I used a professional border around all of the documents included in this mailing.

# THE SPIRIT OF PUBLISHING | Publishing Checklist

**SETS**
Spiritually Enlightening Thoughts™
**Teaching Children How To Connect With God**
Shirley Hildreth

**Category**
**(BISG Major subjects):** Religion (adult)/Family and Relationships/Self-Help
**Edition:** First Edition
**Specifications:** Soft cover; 7" x 9"; 128 pages; illustrated
**Season:** Winter, 2003
**Price:** $19.95
**ISBN No.:** 0-9740500-0-8
**LOC Control No.:** 2003094617
**Intended Audience:** Parents, clergy and teachers of children in a religious setting, extended family members, psychologists, and caregivers of children.
**Promotional Plans:** Author tour, space advertising, direct mail, writer's conferences
**Distribution:** Ingram Book Group
**Trademarks:** *SETS: Spiritually Enlightening Thoughts and Muse Imagery* are trademarks of Muse Imagery LLC, a Nevada Limited Liability Co.
**Description:** *SETS Teaching Children To Connect With God* is a book about a teaching method called Spiritually Enlightening Thoughts (SETS)™ and builds on the premise that thoughts precede actions and that God-based thoughts bring about God-based actions. It shares anecdotes to help the reader understand their role in teaching children this most valuable lesson, and provides teaching modules to enable them to do so.

The reader is invited to slow down and change focus to look for a spiritual meaning and purpose to life then share what they have learned with a child. It speaks of the great potential of each child, and the child that lives within each of us, no matter what their circumstances, and how we, as adults, must nurture this potential so that it will blossom and flourish. The book is non-denominational.

MUSE IMAGERY™
9811 W. Charleston Blvd. Suite 2390
Las Vegas, NV 89117-7915
Phone 702-233-5910
Fax 702-233-1762
marketing@MUSEimagery.com

# THE SPIRIT OF PUBLISHING | Publishing Checklist

## MUSE IMAGERY PUBLISHING PRESENTS

| | |
|---|---|
| **Title:** | SETS Teaching Children How To Connect With God |
| **Author:** | Shirley Hildreth |
| **Retail Price:** | $19.95 |
| **Distribution:** | Ingram Book Group |
| **Discount:** | 55% |
| **ISBN No.:** | 0-9740500-0-8 |
| **LOC Control No.:** | 2003094617 |
| **Edition:** | First Edition |
| **Binding Type:** | Perfect |
| **No. Pages:** | 128; illustrated |
| **Season:** | Winter, 2003 |
| **Category** | |
| **(BISG Major subjects):** | Religion (adult)/Family and Relationships/Self-Help |

**Intended Audience:** Parents, clergy and teachers of children in a religious setting, extended family members, psychologists, and caregivers of children.

**Promotional Plans:** Author tour, space advertising, direct mail, writer's conferences

**Trademarks:** SETS: Spiritually Enlightening Thoughts and Muse Imagery are trademarks of Muse Imagery LLC, a Nevada Limited Liability Company

**Endorsements:** Mark Andrews, Emmy Award winning photographer
(back cover) Roberta and Richard VandeVoort, Marriage and Family Therapists

**Description:** SETS instructs the reader how to teach the most important lesson they will ever teach a child. This proven method builds on the premise that thoughts precede actions and that God-based thoughts bring about God-based actions. It invites the reader to slow down, change focus and look for a spiritual meaning and purpose to life, then share what they have learned with a child. Detailed teaching modules are provided to enable them to do so. Anecdotes are also included to emphasize the great potential of each child.

As this book demonstrates, SETS once learned, will play a vital role in the lives of children who will be expected, with honor and unflinching resolve, to play leading roles in the future of our communities. SETS is non-denominational.

**Forthcoming Books By The Author:**
*SETS Musings Of The Spirit*
*SETS I Know You're There!*
*SETS A Glimpse Of Heaven*

MUSE IMAGERY • 9811 W. Charleston Blvd. Suite 2390 • Las Vegas, NV 89117

| THE SPIRIT OF PUBLISHING | Publishing Checklist |

## Muse Imagery Facsimile Transmittal Sheet

To:      Shauna L. Jones                              From:
       Marketing Director
       MUSE IMAGERY
Fax Number:     702-123-4567
Phone Number:  702-123-4567
E-Mail:          marketing@museimagery.com

                                             Total number of pages 1

**Re: BOOK REVIEW ACKNOWLEDGMENT**

We have received the book review galley(s) for:  ***SETS™ Teaching Children How To Connect With God.***

® We expect to review this book on _____
® We expect to review this book, however the exact date is uncertain at this time.
® Please send photograph of book.      E-mail Address _____
® Please send photograph of author.    E-mail Address _____
® We are sorry, we did not find your book suitable for review at this time.

Additional Comments:
_____
_____
_____
_____
_____

MUSE IMAGERY • 9811 W. Charleston Blvd. Suite 2390 • Las Vegas, NV 89117

# The Spirit of Publishing / Tom Bird

# Step Three: The Initial Contact Phase 3

**Goal: Seeing Who Is Interested in Your Project and Gauging How Interested They Are.**

# INTRODUCTION

Okay, now that you are armed with the essential working knowledge of what it is that you really want to write, as well as being appraised of what options exist for you to get your work into print, it's time to begin projecting it into the marketplace.

As will be elaborately illustrated, our goal is not to catapult you to publication. That comes later. My goal, instead, is to first show you how to acquire those essential offers from necessary literary sources who want to review your work, the step most often overlooked by would-be authors.

I will cover in Chapter Three, the simple truth behind why most writers fail at publication. In Chapter Four, I will detail for you the proper composition of the *Query Letter Package*. If you have created one of these on your own before and you have met with little or no success, you may want to pay extra special atten-

*"You can't change the music of your soul."*
Katharine Hepburn

tion to this chapter. The first line of publication begins with a properly written and circulated *Query Letter Package*. Quite frankly, anyone can receive the acceptances they crave if he or she just follows through on the steps outlined in this chapter.

Chapter Five follows that up by showing you whom to submit your work to, and how. You'll be met with a few surprises here as well.

In Chapter Six, I have included a specific section on collaborative agreements, which describes the contractual obligations that make up one of the industry's quickest and most profitable ways to get published. Of course, if the basis of this chapter doesn't interest you in the least, don't feel bad about skipping it.

*"Man's main task in life is to give birth to himself, to become what he potentially is."*
— Erich Fromm

# Chapter Three: Dodging the Third Critical Error
## Most Writers Make

Let's say that it's Christmas Day or Hanukkah. You've taken weeks to prepare a spread that should grace the cover of *Holiday Meals Magazine*. Everyone is there, dozens of close friends and family who have come in from all across the globe.

Smiling from ear to ear, you are just about to proudly present the food to your cherished, famished herd, when the doorbell rings. Thinking that it may be a late-arriving guest, you rush over, open the door, and find me, whom you have never seen before, standing there, toothy grin, hair flowing way beyond my shoulders, with arched collar, black leather jacket, and all.

Expecting Uncle Hank or Bud, Aunt Vi or someone else you love and adore to be making a last-minute, surprise appearance, you are caught

> *"A problem is a chance for you to do your best."*
> Duke Ellington

completely off guard by me, the stranger at the door. As a result, you don't really know what to say.

"*Ah, yes,*" you mumble under your breath, "*may I help you?*"

"Yes," I reply, as cocky and confident as can be. *"The reason that I am here,"* I say, reaching for your arm, *"is because I would like you to leave with me immediately to do 50 hours of free, physical labor."*

You don't know what to say, but you're sure as heck that you don't want to go. So, you pull back, utter a few polite apologies, and softly close the door in my face.

You then turn, relief gracing your face, and head back to reignite the festivities simply with the glow of your personality, when the doorbell rings again. You slowly and reluctantly turn back and peek out of the peephole in the door to see me standing there again, only this time, there's now a dozen long-haired, smiling, at least slightly warped, literary types, all looking straight toward you, mouthing the same exact request I had beseeched upon you only moments before.

Somehow, you dodge the bullet again, only to be called to the threshold of your home every five minutes by an even larger gathering of persons, looking like me and all mouthing the same request. Eventually, you lose it. Maybe you start screaming obscenities. Maybe you call the cops. Either way, you find yourself responding completely out of character.

What does a scenario such as this have to do with your publishing aspirations as a would-be author?

Everything.

---

*"Aim for success, not perfection. Never give up your right to be wrong, because then you will lose the ability to learn new things and move forward in your life. Remember that fear always lurks behind perfectionism. Confronting your fears and allowing yourself the right to be human can, paradoxically, make you a far happier and more productive person."*
— Dr. David M. Burns

You see, were you to follow the normal procedure subscribed to by most new writers, you'd wind up experiencing the same fate as my friends and me camped out on your lawn. The last thing that an editor or literary agent wants to see appear on his or her desk is an unrequested, full-length manuscript from an unrecognized, new author. The reality is that there is barely time for editors and agents to read the books that they are contractually obligated to review.

## The Simple Truth

As successful as the majority of aspiring authors happen to be in the other aspects of their lives, few, if any, proceed beyond their mistake of sending their hard-earned manuscript off to a publishing house, which is almost certain to reject it. Yet unbeknownst to them, the roots of their rejections spring not from the quality or lack of quality of their work, but instead from violating a simple but essential, unwritten etiquette of the literary world.

Let's frame this situation in a real-life context so as to better help you understand. If you wanted to land a job with a well-thought-of company or corporation, you couldn't expect much, if any, success if you just walked into their headquarters and demanded a high-ranking, executive position or any other job. In most cases, if you were to do that you would be lucky just to be thrown out onto the street. Wouldn't it make sense that if you were to emulate the same action in the literary arena by firing off your manuscript to a publishing house without first going

*"It's not the most difficult thing to know one's self, but the most inconvenient."*
                                        Josh Billings

*"Everything I did in my life that was worthwhile I caught hell for."*

Earl Warren

through the proper channels, that you would meet with the same results? Of course.

So to best dodge such an unnecessary rejection, wouldn't it make sense that maybe you should follow a system comparable to the one utilized in the job placement field? Of course.

In most cases, when you apply for a job you are expected to submit a personal letter and resume'. The literary arena has its own version of that as well. However, in the literary marketplace, rarely is its version sent directly to potential publishers. Because of the usually high traffic volume, it is instead sent to an essential middleman who fills the same role as a headhunter or job placement counselor, called a literary agent.

# Chapter Four: The Writer's Resumé:
## The Query Letter Package

The query letter package is analogous to the use of a resumé in the job market. Just as a resumé secures a job interview, the *Query Letter Package* secures a literary interview with an editor or agent for your work. This point is important enough to be made again: A *Query Letter Package* doesn't sell one's work; it simply gives a writer the opportunity he or she needs to sell his or her work. That's all.

Using it greatly increases your chance of a sale. Ignoring it vastly increases your chance of failure. In fact, inappropriately introducing yourself and your idea to a potential source by sending your manuscript directly will almost certainly lead to rejection. So, if you've been impatiently contemplating saying, *"To hell with the query letter,"* and just submitting the manuscript you've

*"Avoiding danger is no safer in the long run than exposure."*
Helen Keller

written, don't do it. No matter how good your material is, you'll only be setting yourself up for failure.

*The Query Letter Package allows you to gauge the depth of any potential interest in a project.*
If you send out a query and find there is enough interest in your project to devote your time, energy, and potentially money to it, great! If there isn't much or any interest, the query letter can save you from wasting any further resources.
Positive responses derived from your *Query Letter Package* build confidence in your project and your approach to your writing.
This added confidence will not only show itself in your writing style, but the savvy with which you approach the publishing of your material.

*The Query Letter Package enables you to get the professional assistance you may need, which vastly increases your chance of a sale.*
Contrary to popular belief, writing is a team sport. Many people are directly involved in the publishing and success of any project. In the case of a book, for example, anywhere from 12 to 20 highly skilled and artistically inclined individuals directly aid the author in bringing an idea to fruition. Thus it's best to get the input of other potential members of your team as soon as possible.

*The Query Letter Package prevents creative constipation.*
That's right, creative constipation. If you're

*"Push on – keep moving."*
Thomas Morton, 1797

anything like me, and I have to believe that you are, ideas are probably flowing through your mind all the time. If you don't find some way to release them, they'll get backed up. As a result, you'll lose your ability to identify what your creative mind is trying to share with you. You'll get frustrated and angry, negatively reinforcing any output from your creative mind and severely preventing its future attempts to communicate with you.

By properly utilizing a query letter, which is relatively easy to write once you get the hang of it, you will be putting those ideas to use, freeing yourself of the dreaded creative constipation.

*Sending a Query Letter Package is FUN.*
There is no pressure involved. If whomever you contact likes your idea...great! Then, and only then, shall you give serious consideration to actually producing your product. If they don't like your idea, you can either review your query letter and send it elsewhere or dump the idea. Besides a small amount of your time, a few stamps, a bit of stationery, and a few envelopes, you don't have much to lose.

*"Our necessities are few but our wants are endless."*
Josh Billings

# THE QUERY LETTER
## THE TWO TYPES OF QUERY LETTERS

You will send a query letter for Fiction or Non-Fiction. There is no special design that needs to be adhered to for any other or different compartments of writing. What you are writing is either fiction or non-fiction. Period. Though both the fiction and non-fiction query letters are made up of five separate parts, each one has its own unique design.

## THE MOST IMPORTANT ELEMENTS TO KEEP IN MIND ABOUT THE QUERY LETTER:

- *The query should always be neatly typed.*
- *Limit the query to one page in length.*
- *Limit the size of your paragraphs, giving it the appearance of a quick, easy read.*
- *Include your name, address, and telephone number in the upper left-hand corner, in case your query gets separated from your cover letter.*

# THE FIVE ELEMENTS OF A FICTION QUERY LETTER

## 1. THE TITLE

Most new writers erroneously spend far too much time choosing a title for their project. They innocently believe that whatever title they commit to for their query will eventually become the title of their book, which is not true. In fact, it is not unusual for a title to change several times before a final choice is made. Professionals in the literary business are well aware of this, so they won't hold you to any of your initial impulses.

For the purpose of a query letter, it is essen-

> *"Man's main task in life is to give birth to himself, to become what he potentially is."*
> — Erich Fromm

tial that the title merely attract a reader's interest. That's all. Just come up with something that will grab your potential reader's attention.

## 2. The Grabber

The Grabber comprises the first paragraph of a fictional query letter. It should be no more than three short sentences in length. Its purpose is to further entice the reader to review the remainder of your query. No matter how good your query may get later, if you lose an editor or agent here, they won't read the rest of your query. Your work will thus be returned to you without ever having gotten a fair chance to be seen.

Here are three suggestions to better aid you in this area.

**First**: stay away from beginning a query letter with a question. Your readers simply won't know enough about your characters or your story in general to care about the answer to your question.

**Second**: the key to effective fiction is to get your readers to feel. Thus, the best way to grab their attention is to appeal to as many of their five senses as possible. Create an interesting image for your readers to get lost in, and you will have them hooked.

**Third**: to give your readers a better idea of the potential of your work, compare the eventual success of your proposed project with a literary success. See the sample query letter on page 58 to see how this is done.

*"If you want to win anything – a race, your self, your life – you have to go a little berserk."*
George Sheehan

### 3. THE CHARACTERS

Before you can share anything with your agent, editor, or publisher about your proposed work, it is essential that you first identify your top 2-3 characters. Your goal with each character description is to: a) create the proper imagery to bring the character to light in your reader's mind, and b) to begin to gently introduce the story line or plot of your prospective work.

### 4. THE PLOT OR STORY LINE

The next portion of your query should be used to share your plot or story line with the reader.

### 5. THE ENDING

Use the last paragraph to leave your prospective audience with something to remember you and/or your project by.

---

*"Forget goals. Value the progress."*

Jim Bouton

# THE WRITER'S RESUMÉ

## SAMPLE FICTION QUERY LETTER

Author's Name
Author's Address
City, State, Zip

(123)123-1234                                                        email@ambassu.net

May 4, 2002

    Ah! That beloved breed of citizens known as the South Florida retiree. They add just the right touch of annoyance to a non-senior's life by filling up restaurants for the early bird specials, bringing traffic to a crawl by careening down the interstate at the speed limit, and slowing down the checkout lines as they fight for their senior citizen discounts. What a wonderfully predictable life the over-sixty crowd lives, but not Sam and Max. These beautiful and energetic sixty-two-year-old twins are anything but retiring.

    When George, their fellow Ocean Manor resident, is found floating face down in his backyard pool, they're convinced that it wasn't the news that got him down: It was murder. Lieutenant Wayne was unwilling to listen to their theory and their husbands were sorry they did, but Sam and Max were undeterred. Enlisting the aid of the widow Helga and her nerdy accountant Norman, the twins set out to solve the crime with hilarious consequences, proving that *Retirement Can Be Murder*.

    After fifteen years in the college classroom, the list of students I would like to strangle increases daily, but I decided that the safer kind of murder is on paper. Being a professor, my whole working life is nothing but deadlines. No one can hound you more mercilessly than a student waiting for his or her grade. Besides the deadlines associated with a teaching position, I've completed assignments for various academic publishers producing test banks, instructor's manuals, and textbook reviews.

    *Retirement Can Be Murder* is a completed manuscript and can be supplied upon request. I look forward to hearing from you.

Thank you for your consideration,

Lucille Genduso

# The Five Elements of a Non-Fiction Query Letter

## 1. The Title

The purpose and reason behind the title in a non-fiction query letter is exactly the same as its fictional counterpart. It is meant to attract attention. It need not necessarily be considered your final title. In fact, what you choose as your title at this stage will probably change several times before your work appears in print. So, don't place undue pressure upon yourself by sweating over a title. Come up with something appropriate that attracts a reader's attention and go with that.

## 2. The Grabber

Catch your reader's attention with a comparison-evoking statement as was alluded to in the description of the fictional query letter. An example of this technique can be found in the sample non-fiction query letter as well.

## 3. Secondary Markets

Where good imagery catches a reader's attention in a fictional query letter, the identification of a significant population that would be interested in reading your work, how large that audience is, and what void in the literary world you will be filling with your project, does it in the non-fiction query letter. Besides your primary

> *"As Miss America, my goal is to bring peace to the entire world and then to get my own apartment."*
>
> Jay Leno

audience, list anyone you think would be interested in reading about your topic.

## 4. THE MAKEUP AND DESIGN OF YOUR PROJECT

This is where you give agents, editors, and publishers a quick but enlightening rundown of some of the chapter headings, sectional breakdowns, and topics to be covered in your work.

## 5. THE ENDING

As with the fictional query letter, leave your readers with something favorable by which to remember you and/or your project.

*"In no other period of history were the learned so mistrustful of the divine possibilities in man as they are now."*
Gopi Krishna

## SAMPLE NON-FICTION QUERY LETTER

Agent's Name
Agent's Company
Address
City, State, Zip

Dear (Agent's Name),

By 1997 forty percent of the women in the United States were considered obese. Twenty-five percent of the world's population is now considered overweight, and the numbers are continually on the rise. Yet, most diet and health plans on the market today are pure science and don't speak effectively to the underlying problems that actually cause excessive eating, or help before the hand reaches for food.

I have written a book called *I'm in Here Somewhere, One Woman's Path to Peace and Preparation for Weight Loss.* This book builds upon and goes beyond other books written about weight loss and diets.

The audience for this book is vast because it includes not only the tens of millions of obese individuals worldwide, but the even greater numbers of individuals who the obese directly affect, such as friends, family, and health professionals.

I am well known in my field, receive many accolades, and have many accomplishments, but none compare to the peace and progress I now have experienced through my weight loss program.

My manuscript is complete. If you would like to see some of my material, or if you have any questions, feel free to call collect at my home at 123/123-4567 or contact me by e-mail at my_email@aol.com.

Best regards,

## Salutations and Such

Personalize your approach with either type of query by using the name of the literary agent, agency, magazine, or publisher. Sign off at the bottom in your usual manner and by promising to provide anyone interested in seeing more material with whatever they request.

## Credentials

Don't jam up your query letter with a long listing of credits, degrees, and credentials, if you have any. Simply list any pertinent degrees in your letterhead and quickly mention any credits or credentials in no more than a sentence or two at the conclusion of your letter.

## This Decision Is an Easy One to Make

It's decision-making time, but, as you will see, a very easy one to make. What you need to do before moving on is to decide which one of two potential methods available you will choose to employ to submit your query letter package.

The first alternative is to send your material via the old US Post Office, or commonly referred to by those in the cyber world as snail mail. In this regard, snail mail translates to individually addressing each of your 200 or more letters, indi-

*"Blessed is that man who has found his work."*
— Elbert Hubbard

vidually labeling them, stuffing them, and purchasing both mailing postage and return postage for each source chosen. So, not only is it monetarily expensive, but it could take dozens of hours to complete as well.

Now, up until just a few months after 9/11, that was about your only alternative. But then, during those months when the publishing/literary industry almost completely shut down, something changed in the psyches of literary agents everywhere. That is when, in greater numbers than ever before, agents became open to accepting e-mailed query letter packages.

Even though I was thrilled when this trend finally appeared, I was still a bit skeptical. So, I e-mailed several query letters to insure that this trend was indeed real and here to stay. To my amazement, not only was the percentage of positive replies to the query letters nearly eight times higher than what I would have normally expected to receive via snail mailed versions, but on an average over 60% of those contacted replied within 48 hours.

So, your choice is really clearcut. Choosing your literary agents from a database and e-mailing them out takes about 20 minutes as opposed to an average of 18-20 hours via the snail mail route. Outside the purchase of the database listing (and you would have to acquire some sort of listing for the snail mail route as well), it costs absolutely nothing to mail out your 200+ queries. Going the snail mail route, with return postage included, will cost you $148 to send out 200 queries. Response time? You'll begin receiving responses within hours via the e-mail alternative and will have the vast majority of your replies

*"Never put off till tomorrow what you can do today."*
Proverb

back in your hands in days. The snail mail approach? It will take you an average of 6-8 weeks before you can count on having received the majority of your replies.

Now, I realize that there are some of you who still do not feel comfortable with using the computer, let alone the Internet. But the e-mail alternative is just so much faster, more efficient, cheaper, and more successful that I cannot help but highly recommend it. If you don't yet feel comfortable with your computer or the Internet, why not have a friend or a family member who is a bit more cyber savvy submit your package for you? Or, if you would like, we will do it for you. Check out the last few pages of this book for more information.

*"Procrastination is the thief of time."*

Edward Young

# SNAIL MAIL

If I haven't thoroughly convinced you of the value of e-mailing your queries, make sure to include a stamped, self-addresssed envelope, if you decide to use snail mail.

# The Spirit of Publishing / Tom Bird

# Chapter Five: Whom to Submit Your Work to <u>and How</u>

## Let the Author Beware

The good news is that there are thousands of independent firms in this country who claim to perform the services of literary agents.

The bad news is that even though there are a few governing bodies that attempt to do so, there is no universally accepted body of ethics, like the American Medical Association for the medical field, that determines who is and who is not qualified to be a literary agent. What this means, in my estimation, is that over three-quarters of those individuals who call themselves literary agents fall way short of the title, or in the worst of cases, are downright frauds.

> *"My choice early in life was either to be a piano player in a whorehouse or a politician. And to tell the truth, there's hardly any difference."*
> 
> Harry S. Truman

> "The great thing in this world is not so much where we are, but in what direction we are moving."
> — Oliver Wendell Holmes

## How Can You Tell?

A literary agent is **First** a commission-based salesperson.

**Second**, he or she has the expertise to help you edit and refine your writing for submission to publishing houses.

**Third**, literary agents fill the role of literary legal counsel. He or she negotiates and enforces your literary contracts.

How do you know whether an agent is a potential fraud? Quite simply, if they charge for any of the above services, be very, very leery.

Let's take that point a little further.

Let us say that a perspective agent's name is Bob. Bob has expressed an interest in reviewing your manuscript for potential representation to a publisher.

Bob reminds you, however, *"Don't forget to send along the $1200 reading fee with your manuscript."*

Many so-called literary agents charge reading fees, not because they are paying an outside service to review your material but instead to subsidize their incomes because they are not making enough money, if any, selling works to publishers. What then does that tell you about Bob's ability as a literary salesperson? Right. He has little, if any, and he certainly is not the type of person you want handling your literary gem, no matter how vulnerable and idealistic you may be.

The same goes with editing fees.

The biggest come-on of the latter part of the last century in the literary industry was staged when a number of so-called editing services began contacting literary agents with an offer many of the latter couldn't refuse. Since the once-unsuspecting audience of aspiring authors had begun to catch on to the *reading fee game,* these editing agencies decided to offer teetering agencies an opportunity to significantly subsidize their meager incomes. All these agencies had to do was recommend the services of the editing firm. If a referral from one of the agencies signed on with the editorial firm, the agency was given anywhere from a 30-40% kickback from the fees charged by the editing service.

Pretty sweet deal, huh? For the indiscreet agency and editing service maybe, but not for the innocent writer who in most cases was led to believe, by the agency, that all that was needed to achieve publication was one, good, thorough edit. Unfortunately though, even if that were the case, that would have been impossible with any of the aforementioned firms, who in most cases used high school seniors and college underclassmen to revise and edit the manuscripts they received.

*"Give them great meals of beef and iron and steel, they will eat like wolves and fight like devils."*
Shakespeare

# WHERE TO FIND THAT RIGHT AGENT

There are plenty of listings of literary agents available.

- **The Literary Marketplace** *(LMP): The Directory of the American Book Publishing Industry, as it is referred to by*

> "Successful people are the ones who can think up things for the rest of the world to keep busy at."
>
> Don Marquis

its publisher, can be found in almost any library. Though it offers the names, addresses, and telephone numbers, as well as a small description of approximately 200 literary agents, the majority of the information on each literary agent is meant for use by proven professionals within the field. Thus, the descriptions are often of little use to the new writer.

- **The Writer's Market,** *by Writer's Digest Books: This publication offers a listing of approximately 100 literary agents.*

- **Independent Listings**: *Libraries often carry general listings of literary agents that have been published over the years. But oftentimes the addresses and telephone numbers listed in such publications are outdated, so check carefully.*

- **Tom Bird's Selective Guide to Literary Agents Database**: *Specifically designed for use by the new author, it boasts a listing of over 400 top literary agents who don't charge fees and who are open to accepting new clients. For your convenience and in an effort to save you time and money, the Literary Guide is offered as a database only.*

# How to Choose That Right Agent

The acquisition of the proper literary representative is paramount to your success in this field. Allow me to STRESS again, that it is of the utmost importance to find the right literary agent for YOU.

Each literary agent is different. Each one has different qualities, likes, dislikes, and approaches. As with any partnership, the right literary agent will make you. The wrong one can break you. Thus it is important that you don't just take the first literary agent that happens along and offers you representation. No. It is important that your decision for the choice of a literary agent be based upon a significant amount of comparative research.

To evaluate a literary agent for contact, you should consider each of the following:

- **Area of Expertise**: Do they handle the type of material you want to write?
- **Are They Taking on New Clients?**: If they are not willing to take on anyone new, there's no reason to even contact them.
- **Versatility**: How many different types of books a literary agent represents is very important. For example, if you choose an agent who only works with romance novels, and then after he or she sells your first Harlequin you get an impulse to write a cookbook, you will have to go outside your present agent for representation.
- **Contacts**: Does the agent or agents you are considering have developed contacts at the major publishing houses?

*"I don't want the cheese, I just want to get out of the trap."*
Spanish Proverb

- **Commission Rate**: What commission rate do they charge? Ten percent or 15?

- **Clout**: Do they represent important writers so publishers pay attention to them? What new clients do they represent?

- **Sales Ratio**: This information is hard to come by, but if you can acquire it, it will prove the most beneficial of all criteria considered. Defined, a sales ratio for a literary agent is simply the number of books sold per year per client. If a literary agent has 30 clients and sold 15 books last year, he or she averages one-half of a book sale per year per client represented, which is an outstanding ratio.

- **Size**: Small literary agents, 50 clients and under, are oftentimes new in the business, hungrier, and willing to offer you more of their time than larger agents, 150 clients and above. But the presence of larger, older, and, thus, more established agents usually have an inside track.

- **Location**: To be able to have a profitable working relationship with a literary agent, it is important that you are able to get along with them. A specific location oftentimes determines a person's attitude and approach to life. At times, location also determines specialty. Make sure that you strongly consider this when shopping for an agent.

> "Man is his own star, and the soul that can render an honest and perfect man commands all light, all influence, all fate."
> John Fletcher 1647

# Finding a Literary Agent for Your Book

## Step One

Go to one (or more than one) of the listings of literary agents mentioned in this chapter. Then, based upon the criteria which was shared with you in that same section, choose at least 200 agencies (remember it is essential to be thorough to be successful in this arena) that you feel, for one reason or another, would be valid representatives for you. Then, based upon what you learned from reading their descriptions, and even more so on how you intuitively feel about each one, arrange your listing from the literary agent you think would be best for you to the one you feel would be the least best for you.

## Step Two

Forward your *Query Letter Package* to the bottom third of your listing. Then sit back and wait for their replies. Once you receive your first offer to review your work, which is our goal for this section, send your *Query Letter Package* out to the remaining agents on your list.

If you do not receive any offers to review your work from your first mailing, take a look at your responses. Do they say something to you? Are you doing something incorrectly? If so, make the proper adjustments, and forward your *Query Letter Package* to the next third. Then patiently wait for their responses. Once you get an offer

*"While one person hesitates because he feels inferior, the other is busy making mistakes and becoming superior."*
— Henry C. Link

> *"Every man has the right to risk his own life in order to save it."*
> Jean-Jacques Rousseau

from an agency to review your work, submit your *Query Letter Package* to the rest of the literary agents on your list. If you don't get any acceptances, which would be very unusual, then go over your responses again to see if you can improve your approach before sending your package out again.

This system, like everything offered in this book, is designed to allow you to learn and grow as you go. If, for example, you were to submit a flawed *Query Letter Package* to your entire listing all at once, all of them would probably reject your work. You would have wasted your entire listing, and learned nothing more than what it is to be a frustrated writer. But the staggered submission system saves you from all that. As a result, the lessons you learn propel you rapidly in the direction of your eventual success, as opposed to just further frustrating your efforts.

After the sale of your first work, you will have established yourself as a commodity. You will have value and will have garnered valuable exposure to the literary marketplace. You will come in contact with other agents and have editors who will offer you recommendations for representatives if you need them. At that point, it will be relatively simple to acquire the services of an agency, so you only have to go through this elaborate but exciting process for the sale of your first book.

## STEP THREE

Wait. After you've received your first offer to review, the next step is just to sit back and collect acceptances, or work on another *Query Letter Package* in a non-competing field. There's nothing else that can be done until you have heard, whether they replied affirmatively or not, from at least 75% of your sources.

# Querying Magazine Articles, Short Stories, and Poetry

Since most literary agents do not represent articles, short stories, and poetry, it is common practice to submit your *Query Letter Package* directly to the editor of a publication unless the magazine, or whomever you are approaching, has on staff a *submissions* or *acquisitions editor* or a specialty editor who would be in charge of reviewing your type of material.

## Finding Sources

Where can you find a listing of sources that you can approach with your ideas for a magazine article or short story? Here are a few suggestions:

- **A Newsstand**: *This is the best place to go when researching sources for your article and short story ideas. Not only can you catch a glimpse of the publication or publications you will be approaching, but you can also copy down the correct name and*

*"We don't receive wisdom; we must discover it for ourselves after a journey that no one can take for us or spare us."*
Marcel Proust

address of the appropriate contact in each case. In a business with a high turnover rate like the magazine field, this is a necessity.

- **Writer's Digest**, *by Writer's Digest Books: This publication boasts hundreds of potential sources for your work. However, because of the high turnover referred to above, oftentimes your potential editors may have left for another position elsewhere, the magazine may have gone out of business, or the magazine could have completely changed focus, making any possible submission a sure reject. That's why the newsstand approach is such a strongly suggested mode of gathering sources. Using that technique, your information will always be in its most present, up-to-date form.*
- **The Writer's Handbook**, *by The Writer Inc.: This publication houses a smaller listing than its competitor posted directly above, with many of the same drawbacks.*

## SUBMITTING QUERIES FOR MAGAZINE ARTICLES, SHORT STORIES, OR POETRY

As with books, it is essential that you utilize a multiple submissions system. First, arrange your potential sources from who would pay you the most for a prospective piece to who would pay you the least. If you don't know what a specific publication would pay you, call and ask them, or use a SASE and send for a copy of their writer's

*"The very purpose of existence is to reconcile the glowing opinion we hold of ourselves with the appalling things that other people think about us."*
Quentin Crisp

guidelines. Calling is quicker, but occasionally you may find yourself caught in an awkward position by doing so.

After you've properly arranged your sources, send to the few top-paying sources first, giving them at least four weeks to respond. Then send to the next highest paying group, allowing them the same amount of time to reply, before approaching your remaining sources.

Why do you go to your best paying sources first? The answer is simple. You just want to allow those sources that can offer you the most money, as well as the highest degree of exposure (the two usually go hand in hand), the first opportunity to publish your work. By starting at the bottom, you may be selling yourself short by potentially keeping your work from being published by a much better paying source.

*"Only the curious will learn and only the resolute overcome the obstacles of learning. The quest quotient has always excited me more than the intelligence quotient."*
— Eugene S. Wilson

## A Special Note on Poetry

If you are sending off a *Query Letter Package* to approach potential sources about a book of poetry, follow the design described above for a non-fiction *Query Letter Package*.

# Commonly Asked Questions About Query Submissions

*What about those sources that accept completed works? Should I still query them?*

Yes. By always sending your *Query Letter Package* first, you will be able to acquire important preliminary information concerning your source's reaction to your ideas. Following this procedure will afford you the opportunity to modify and appropriately adjust your work before submitting it for review. Thus always sending your *Query Letter Package* first will increase your chance of an eventual sale.

*Should we write to or adjust to a specific market?*

Write what you feel most comfortable writing, no matter what genre or area of writing that may be. That's the only way that you will be able to continue to write and, thus, succeed. Learn from your mistakes and adjust to the specific requirements of individual markets, but don't compromise by writing something that you have no desire to be associated with. Write what is in your heart and to the market that is most suitable for your form of expression. Compromising oneself leads you away from the areas in which you will write best, and, thus, deters your efforts toward publication.

*Should query letters be sent out before a project is complete?*

If you do not have a completed manuscript, I suggest you employ the methods I share in my book *Your Artist Within*. which will enable you to complete your book in 90 days or less. Then, send out your *Query Letter Package*. However, having a completed manuscript in hand before sending out your query is not a necessity, even though it does work to your advantage.

*"To love what you do and feel that it matters – how can anything be more fun?"*
Katherine Graham

# WHOM TO SUBMIT YOUR WORK TO AND HOW

*What if I've already completed a manuscript?*

Bravo! To have already completed a manuscript without gathering the necessary confirmations one gets from a *Query Letter Package* says a lot of great things about you.

The drawback is that it will make your query letter a little more difficult to write (you'll probably feel as if you're being asked to shrink your entire book into one page), but just follow the same procedures that I outlined earlier, then be ready to make whatever changes are necessary to your manuscript before submitting it.

*How do I protect my work from being stolen?*

Before I begin to address how to protect your work, it is important for you to understand that you cannot copyright an idea. This means that if you submit a *Query Letter Package* for review, you can only copyright the *Query Letter Package* and not the idea that it represents.

So, what do you do? Simple. Though it is my opinion that work is very rarely stolen within this business (the risks are just too high), it is very simple to protect anything that you've written. You can do so in one of two ways.

**First**, you yourself copyright your book, or with the assistance of an attorney, through The Library of Congress. Doing it yourself will cost you around $30. All you have to do is contact The Library of Congress in Washington, D.C. to get all the appropriate forms. Of course, if you go through an attorney, you will have to pay legal fees to get your copyright.

**Second**, you can simply utilize The Common Copyright Law. How do you do that? All you have to do is send out a copy of your finished product

> *"When a fantasy turns you on, you're obligated to God and nature to start doing it – right away."*
> 
> Stewart Brand

to yourself. When the envelope returns to you, don't open it and just store it in a safe place. If you are ever asked to prove the date of your connection with the material, you will be able to do so just by producing the unopened, postmarked envelope.

*How long do I have to reply to a request to review my material?*
Don't be scared if you receive an acceptance before you have even started working on a project. You'll have plenty of time, usually up to a year, to get back to any interested parties with material. The only thing to keep in mind is that you don't want to let a potential source forget who you are while they are waiting. So give them a call or drop them a line every now and again just to update them on your progress.

---

> "Believe in you and the things you do. You won't go wrong you know. This is our family rule."
> Sister Sledge,
> from their hit: *"We Are Family"*

# Chapter Six: Collaborative Agreements

## The Two Collaborative Routes

As I mentioned in the Introduction to this section, I have included this chapter because it details possibly the most safe, secure, and profitable arena for a new writer to break into the publishing field.

Within this specific field, a writer can choose one of two routes to follow. The first route is that of being a ghostwriter. The second path is that of a co-author. Though the two may sound similar to the novice or non-writer, they are vastly different in structure, design, output, notoriety, and pay.

*"Most people put off till tomorrow that which they should have done yesterday."*
Edgar Watson Howe

### Ghostwriting

By definition, ghostwriters are simply glorified secretaries. That doesn't mean that they are with-

> *"It's an extra dividend when you like the girl you're in love with."*
>
> — Clark Gable

out talent. That just means that they are called upon to use fewer of their abilities than a co-author.

A ghostwriter is usually called in when a celebrity or expert in one field or another has some prepared material, no matter how rough it may be, and is asked to reform it, retype, and edit this gobbledegook into shape. The ghostwriter is usually paid a one-time fee.

And even though a good ghostwriter can oftentimes build up a substantial reputation for himself or herself among his or her peers or among editors in the business, they receive either no, or at best very little, notoriety for their work. Rarely are their names listed alongside that of the celebrity on the cover of the book, they usually don't receive any cut of the royalties, and they are usually given no real credit for any of the success the book eventually experiences.

## Co-Authoring

A co-author actually authors any book they are involved with. As a result, they receive an ample amount of notoriety and are paid a vast amount more than a ghostwriter. Their names are printed alongside that of the celebrity on the cover of the book. They are usually paid a percentage of all revenues generated by the book, and share the copyright with their co-author.

All in all, if you can get it, co-authoring is the best way to go. But don't allow anyone, especially someone who has never done it before, to convince you that it is easy to co-author. To be able to unselfishly capture the voice, tone, and message of your celebrity, you have to give up your own views and biases, incessantly research your subject, and probe the psyche of your celebrity for the truth behind their innermost thoughts and feelings.

Again, it takes a unique person to be able to do this, and editors know that. But the residuals, and the pay, are much better than ghostwriting, if you can make the unselfish adjustments.

At the end of this chapter is a copy of a standard collaborative agreement that I have been using for nearly ten years. Since everything is negotiable in this type of dealing, I simply keep this contract on file in my computer and adjust it to meet each particular situation. If you are interested in entering the field of co-authoring, I suggest that you do the same thing.

All the specific points and paragraphs in the sample collaborative agreement located at the end of this chapter are essential. But since I feel that the majority of the elements in the agreement are self-explanatory, I will only highlight the major points. Each major point and where it can be found in the sample contract is listed as well.

# DUTIES AND RESTRICTIONS: PARAGRAPHS 2, 6, & 11

In any collaborative agreement, it is essential to specifically spell out what each party will be responsible for doing. As a writer, it is also important to make it clear that you will be working on other projects besides the one mentioned in the contract. As far as your celebrity's duties are concerned, make sure he or she commits to reviewing all of your work and all proofs in a timely fashion. Getting a celebrity to commit to a major promotional role shortly after the book is released is also in your best career and financial interests.

*"The ancestor of every action is a thought."*
Emerson

### Title of the Work: Paragraph 3

Co-authors need to share in all major decisions. Thus it is important that both co-authors have a say in the eventual title of the book. Though if it comes down to whether you get the notoriety of your name on the book's cover or an equal say in what the eventual title will be, go for the listing of your name.

### Approval by Celebrity: Paragraph 4

It is extremely important that your celebrity approve anything that you write in their voice. That way they will have to take responsibility for what they say through you, and you will be protected from becoming their scapegoat, if what they have had to say isn't received as well as they expected it to be.

### Preservation of the Celebrity's Rights: Paragraph 5

For the sake of being fair, it is only right that you pledge, as a worthy co-author, not to reveal any secrets or information to outside parties that may be considered private and personal to your celebrity.

### Ownership of Copyright: Paragraph 9

This is always a major negotiation point, because whoever owns the copyright, owns the book. Thus, the owner of the copyright can call the shots on what is done with it.

> *"Capture the moment, whoever you are. None of us is here forever."*
> — Adrian, 1958-1991

## INCOME: PARAGRAPH 10

As a co-author, your biggest concern should always be covering your time and expenses to write a book. So you want to acquire the highest percentage of up-front money possible. The best you can usually hope for when working with a national celebrity is 50%. But, of course, all of this is dependent upon the potential amount of money a project may bring in. Receiving a decent percentage of the total royalty revenue after the up-front money should be viewed as a bonus.

## ARBITRATION: PARAGRAPH 14

Utilizing any other route besides arbitration to dispute a difference between co-authors can take years in court and cost tens of thousands of dollars. Thus it is best for all concerned if you and your co-author agree to settle any disputes between yourselves in arbitration as opposed to an open court setting.

## DEATH AND DISABILITY: PARAGRAPHS 15 & 16

It will be in your best interests if, in the event of the unfortunate death or disability of your co-author, you retain the rights to complete the collaboration. As well, it is in the best interest of your estate that they retain the rights to have the collaborative work completed in your absence if something should happen to you.

## LITERARY AGENT: PARAGRAPH 18

Since you will be the most qualified source in this regard, it is always best if you can choose the

*"Our American professors like their literature clear and cold and pure and very dead."*
Sinclair Lewis

right literary agent for the both of you, with the proper consent of your co-author, of course.

## Governing Law: Paragraph 21

Since the hiring of out-of-town legal counsel cannot only be a major inconvenience but very expensive, the locale in which any disputes between you and your co-author are tried is an important issue.

*"If people can be educated to see the lowly side of their own natures, it may be hoped that they will also learn to understand and to love their fellow man better."*

— Carl Jung

# Sample Collaboration Agreement

COLLABORATION AGREEMENT

AGREEMENT made as of the _____ day of _____, 20____, by and between _____ (hereinafter called "_____") and TOM BIRD of Pittsburgh, Pennsylvania, (hereinafter called "BIRD"):

WHEREAS, the parties desire to collaborate on a project currently untitled, the content of which they agree will concern the views, playing days, coaching days, and life of _____ (hereinafter called the "Work") and to provide for the sale, lease, license, and other disposition of the rights thereto;

NOW, THEREFORE, in consideration of the premise and of the mutual promises and undertakings herein contained, and for other good and valuable consideration, receipt and sufficiency of which is hereby acknowledged, the parties agree as follows:

1. Collaboration. The parties shall make themselves available to each other at times and places mutually agreeable to discuss the Work. They shall collaborate exclusively with each other in, and perform the services necessary for, the preparation and writing of the Work and the publication and promotion of the Work.

2. Duties and Restrictions.
    a. _____ shall cooperate with BIRD in the preparation of an outline of the Work, in the preparation of the entire Work, and in the correction of all proofs of the Work.
    b. BIRD shall be solely responsible for writing the book-length manuscript and for obtaining any and all necessary permissions for use of copyrighted or other proprietary material. BIRD shall prepare and deliver the manuscript of the Work to _____ for _____ approval within a sufficient time to allow _____ to review the Work and to allow BIRD to make any necessary revisions before the manuscript delivery date stipulated in _____ and BIRD's contract with the book publisher. _____ shall revise the text, if necessary, pursuant to _____ recommendations. BIRD and _____ agree to revise the manuscript according to the publisher's reasonable recommendations, if any. BIRD shall deliver the text of the Work to the book publisher in accordance with the publishing schedule, as that may be adjusted or extended from time to time.
    c. The parties agree that both of them will be involved in the negotiation of any contract(s) for publication or for any other exploitation of the Work, that both will be listed as authors on any such contract(s), and that both will execute any such contracts.

3. Title of the Work. The title of the Work in all forms in English throughout the world shall be subject to the express approval of _____ and BIRD.

4. Approval by. Any information concerning the events, persons, facts, circumstances, or stories of his life and career that _____, in his sole judgment, deems confidential shall at all times be treated as such and respected by BIRD. This provision shall survive the termination or expiration of this Agreement.

5. Preservation of Rights. All rights of _____, including rights in his life material, personal performance, and personal appearance rights, or rights to use, reproduce, or represent his likeness, face, voice,

name, or body, in whole or in part, for purposes of personal appearance in film or on stage, endorsements, advertisements, or charitable or educational appearances, or otherwise are reserved by _____, except as are reasonably necessary for the purposes of this Agreement.

  6. BIRD's Duties and Restrictions. _____ acknowledges that BIRD will be engaged in other pursuits during the time he is performing under this Agreement, which pursuits are likely to include authorship of other books, articles, and literary compositions, and that BIRD will not devote his entire time to the purposes of this Agreement. BIRD agrees, however, to diligently apply himself hereunder and to render his best efforts to the purposes of this Agreement. BIRD hereby agrees that he will not, without written permission of _____, publish, authorize, assist in or associate himself editorially or in any other manner with the publication or production, in any form whatsoever, of material based on or incorporating any portion of the events, persons, facts, circumstances, stories, or other material concerning _____ life and career. This provision shall survive the termination and expiration of this Agreement.

  7. Joint Venture. The parties hereby form a joint venture. The parties do not intend by this Agreement to form a partnership between them, nor shall this Agreement be construed to constitute a partnership.

  8. Joint Work. The parties intend that their contributions to the Work be merged into inseparable or interdependent parts of a unitary whole, so that the Work shall be a joint work under Art. 101 of the Copyright Act of 1976 of which the parties shall be co-authors.

  9. Ownership of Copyright. _____ and BIRD shall be joint owners of the copyright in the Work during its initial and any renewal or extended terms, in all forms and all languages throughout the world, and all material prepared in connection with the Work and any registration of copyright in the Work shall be in the names of both _____ and BIRD.

  10. Income. All income accruing from any exploitation of the Work, including any contract with a publisher, shall be divided equally between the parties, up through and including the first $50,000 received from any publisher or other licensee; thereafter, income will be divided at the rate of sixty percent (60%) to _____ and forty percent (40%) to BIRD. All contracts relating to exploitation of the Work shall specify said division of royalties as well as require statements from the payor to each party.

  11. Review of Manuscript and Galleys. The parties agree each will promptly review the copyedited manuscript and galleys.

  12. Indemnity. The parties agree to share equally the authors' responsibilities of warranty and indemnity as expressed in any contract for the exploitation of the Work, including those for reasonable attorneys' fees, except that in any instance where any breach is the result of negligence of one of the parties (including failure to obtain permissions or other unauthorized use of copyrighted material), then such party will be solely responsible for any costs or damages incurred by the Publisher or any licensee of the Work and by the non-responsible party.

  13. Consent for Reuse of Materials. The parties agree that neither will incorporate material based on or derived from the Work in any subsequent work without the consent of the other.

14. Arbitration. Any controversy or claim arising out of or relating to this agreement or any breach thereof shall be settled by arbitration in accordance with the Rules of the American Arbitration Association of the City of Philadelphia, and award rendered by said arbitrators shall be treated as a final and non-appealable judgment of any court having jurisdiction thereof. The preceding sentence shall not apply to disputes concerning the editorial content of the Work.

15. Death or Disability Before Completion of the Manuscript. The death or disability of either _____ or BIRD prior to the completion of the manuscript of the Work shall not terminate this Agreement unless the Work shall become commercially unsaleable thereby. In the event of the death or total disability of BIRD, his personal representatives shall secure, at the expense of BIRD or his estate, a substitute author, acceptable to _____ and to the book publisher, to complete the Work, and BIRD or his estate shall continue to be entitled to all the benefits of this Agreement. In the event BIRD or his estate does not obtain a substitute author acceptable to _____, _____ shall have the right to retain the services of a substitute author of his own choice. In that event, the reasonable compensation to such substitute author for completing the Work shall be deducted from BIRD's share of the income accruing from the exploitation of the Work, and _____, in his sole discretion, shall determine what copyright interest, if any, the substitute author shall receive. In the event of the total disability of _____, _____ shall make his best efforts to provide life materials to BIRD and to accomplish the purposes of this Agreement. In the event of the death of _____, this Agreement will terminate, unless, in the judgment of BIRD and the book publisher, sufficient life materials have been made or can be made available to BIRD so that he can complete the Work, and the Work will be commercially saleable, in which case BIRD may elect to continue this Agreement, and the Agreement shall be binding upon heirs and estates.

16. Death of_____ or BIRD After Completion of the Manuscript. If, after the completion of the Manuscript, BIRD dies, _____ shall have the right alone to negotiate and contract for the publication and other exploitation of the Work; make revisions in any subsequent editions; and generally act with regard thereto as if he were the sole author, except that _____ shall cause BIRD's share of the proceeds as provided in this Agreement to be paid to his estate, and shall furnish to his estate copies of all contracts made by _____ pertaining to the Work. If, after completion of the manuscript, _____ dies, BIRD shall have the right and the obligation to negotiate and contract for the publication and exploitation of rights in the Work, subject to the approval of _____ estate, and he shall cause _____ share of the proceeds as provided in this Agreement to be paid to _____ estate, and shall furnish to _____ estate copies of all contracts pertaining to the Work.

17. Term. This Agreement, unless otherwise terminated under the terms hereof, shall continue for the life of any copyright in the Work and any and all renewals or extensions of said copyright.

18. Literary Agent. Unless otherwise agreed in writing, BIRD will also serve as the exclusive selling agent of the Work, and is expected to diligently and faithfully use all reasonable efforts to effectuate the sale, lease, license, or transfer of rights to the Work.

19. Waiver. Failure on the part of any party to insist upon strict compliance by the other with any term, covenant, or condition hereof shall not be deemed to be a waiver of such term, covenant, or condition.

20. Benefit. This Agreement shall inure to the benefit of, and shall be binding upon, the executors, administrators, heirs, and assigns of the parties.

21. Entire Understanding and Governing Law. This Agreement constitutes the entire understanding of the parties, may be amended or modified only in writing signed by the parties, and shall be governed by the laws of the Commonwealth of Pennsylvania.

22. Counterparts. This Agreement may be signed in two or more counterparts, each of which shall be an original for all purposes.

IN WITNESS WHEREOF, the parties hereunto have set their respective hands and seals as of the day and year first above written.

WITNESS:                                COLLABORATORS

_____                _____


_____                _____

                                        Tom Bird

# SOME EXCERPTS FROM TOM'S GOOD NEWS NEWSLETTER

*Diana T., a Ph.D. who resides in England, received four positive replies this week from literary agents to the query letter package on her first novel. You may remember Diana via my references to her. She wrote approximately the last 25,000 words of her novel in one day.*

*Karen from Memphis has received two positive responses to the query letter on her novel.*

*Lorraine, who lives in Atlanta and is a professor, is now up to approximately 25 positive responses from literary agents to her query letter package. Her book is on a unique inside-outside approach to weight loss and soul retrieval.*

*Dorothy G., from Scottsdale, one of Tom's IWP students, just recently e-mailed her query letter package on her non-fiction book. Within less than seventy-two hours she received four requests from literary agents to see material on her first book, with the first reply being received approximately twelve hours after she sent it.*

*Karen and Chet, also from Scottsdale, have 12 replies to their query letter from literary agents who are asking to see more material. The couple is presently working on compiling the necessary submission package.*

*Michelle from Miami is already up to ten requests from literary agents for more material via her e-mail query letter, and the vast majority of her positive replies came in the first few days after she sent out her package.*

*More good news – Karen from Tom's FAU class has started work on her second book. Her first book has been professionally edited and is on its way to publishers.*

*David, from Virginia, the Reverend of the Barnum and Bailey, reports that he landed an agent from LA for his first book.*

*Suzan, from Sedona, received her first offer of representation from a literary agent for her first book. JET Literary Agency was the happy giver. Suzan was floored.*

# Step Four: Submitting Your Work  4

**Goal for Books:**
**To Receive an Offer of Representation from a Literary Agent**

**Goal for Shorter Pieces:**
**To Receive a Written Contract from a Potential Source**

# INTRODUCTION

In this section, we will cover the essential step that most aspiring authors normally overlook.

Included in this step will not only be the 'hows' and 'whats' of submitting your work, but what you need to know about your associated contractual obligations as well.

If you have arrived at this place after having already submitted your query letter package, you are only one step away from publication. Congratulations.

If you have not yet submitted your query letter package, it's about time you got to it, don't you think?

---

*"In life, as in football, you won't go far unless you know where the goalposts are."*
Arnold Glasow

# Chapter Seven: How to Submit Your Writing

## Submitting Your Book Idea

### Reviewing, Evaluating, and Most of All Standardizing Your Agent Responses

If you have sent out your *Query Letter Packages* on your books and you have begun receiving responses, you have probably already come to an understanding of just how schizophrenic an industry this happens to be.

First, your sources replied in a wide variety of ways, ranging from a neatly typed letter or polite telephone call (telephone calls are very rare and should be taken as a sign directly from God) to sloppily handwritten notes. Second, they probably are far from what you expected them to be.

Still, it is very important to pay very close attention to your immediate reaction to each response, as this will serve as a true and accurate

> "An idea isn't worth much until a man is found who has the energy and ability to make it work."
>
> William Feather

key to help you better understand exactly what type of person, and/or agency, your literary soul is leading you to, or away from.

So, budget some time in a very relaxed space to look over your acceptances. While doing this, on a separate piece of paper, spontaneously list each acceptance offering agency. Then rate your agents, giving each a score from a low of '1' to a high of '10,' based on two factors: their enthusiasm for your work, and how strongly you feel about each one. Then add those two figures together. The sum you come up with will allow you to rank them from whom you like best to whom you like least.

> *"Any activity becomes creative when the doer cares about doing it right, or better."*
> — John Updike

# THE SUBMISSION PACKAGE

Before we go any further, let me first clarify that a submission package, no matter what shape, size, or design it takes, is put together after receiving positive replies to your *Query Letter Package* from a literary agent. If he or she is interested in you and in your work after reviewing your submission package, there is a good chance that you will be offered a contract.

Once that happens, your agent will normally help you refine your submission package for attracting publishers. After that is completed, it is sent off for sale.

The proposal is utilized for non-fiction projects that you cannot assume your readers will have more than a common recognition of. Thus, a more elaborate introduction of the subject matter is needed. This introduction is spread throughout the multitude of variables, which make up the *Proposal Package*.

The thorough introduction of the necessary topic, via a *Proposal Package*, is spread throughout several categories, listed below. Most of these components will be replicated in the other two submission packages, the Synopsis Package, and the Children's Book Package. So, except where a separate clarification and/or introduction is necessary and is included, the description of the majority of the following will transfer, quite nicely, for use in the other areas as well.

1. *A Title Page*
2. *A Table of Contents*
3. *A One-Page Bio on the Author or a Curriculum Vitae*
4. *An Overview or Synopsis, giving a general idea of what is being proposed and why*
5. *A Chapter-by-Chapter Sketch of the book*
6. *A Collection of Sample Work from the book*

To enable you to best understand the elements of these packages, following are more elaborate descriptions of the above elements.

## AUTHOR BIO

The major purpose of the one-page bio is to introduce the author, or authors, of a proposed work to a literary agent. To successfully compose a bio, a few points must always be highlighted.

- *Identify what attributes make you the best writer for this piece.*
- *List any writing or experience credentials you may have garnered that verify some authority in the field you are writing about; or, if neither of those are possible, at least show or illustrate a significant amount of commitment that you have already made to*

*"I am looking for a lot of men who have an infinite capacity to not know what can't be done."*
Henry Ford

*the art of writing, even if that means just having kept a journal for the last 20 years.*

• *Specify the direction of your future interests.*

It is usually best to organize the above into three separate paragraphs. The use of the third person is also highly recommended over first person. It is just much easier to cover large amounts of ground quicker in that manner. It is also essential that the bio you write ooze with your style and character. Don't try to copy anybody here. Cheap impressions never sell in the literary world. Be yourself, and let them see who you are.

## THE OVERVIEW OR SYNOPSIS

In essence, the book overview used for non-fiction, which is composed of the same five components that make up a query, is a long, long query letter designed to entertainingly answer any and all questions that a literary agent could potentially ask. To be an effective writer, it is essential that several topics be approached and expounded upon, most of which should have already been covered in the aforementioned exercise and can be conveniently converted for use in your book overview. They are:

1. What is your idea for a book?

2. Who is your audience?

3. Why will your book be a valuable asset to your audience?

4. What do you hope to accomplish with the writing of your book?

5. What ideas do you have for the potential sale and promotion of the book?

*"Always bear in mind that your own resolution to success is more important than any other one thing."*
Abraham Lincoln

6. How many words do you expect the book to be?

7. What are you willing to do to participate in the promotion of the book?

8. How long will it take you to fully complete the writing of the book?

An example of an overview for your study and review is included in the sample *Proposal Packages* later in this chapter.

Like the book proposal, the synopsis, which is employed for use with fiction, is a long query letter. But it is important that your synopsis successfully achieve two very important goals.

**First** and foremost, the synopsis must carry with it the tone and creative tension of your book. To do this, simply expand the thoroughly shortened story line or plot, the fourth component, that you shared in your query letter. Again, remember, it's important to make your tale come to life by routinely hitting on all of the reader's five senses.

**Second**, it is necessary that the topics listed above for the Overview also be effectively, but not necessarily directly, addressed in the Synopsis.

*"Losers visualize the penalties of failure. Winners visualize the rewards of success."*
    Dr. Rob Gilbert

## THE CHAPTER-BY-CHAPTER SKETCH

The chapter-by-chapter sketch gives a literary agent a more detailed idea of how your book will be composed. The main focus of the chapter-by-chapter sketch is to share enough to give your authoritative reader a developed idea of the content of each chapter without telling him or her so much that it eventually winds up boring them.

## SAMPLE WORK

No matter what you've offered literary agents up to this point in your submission package, how well you pull off this section spells *make it or break it time.*

There are two things that a literary agent will look to discern from any sample chapters that you include. First of all, they will want to see how quickly you grab your reader's attention. Second, they want to see how effectively you communicate and carry your story forward.

## THE PROPOSAL PACKAGE

The *Proposal Package* is normally broken up into the following components:

1. *Title Page*
2. *Table of Contents for the Submission Package*
3. *Overview*
4. *Marketing Sketch*
5. *Chapter-by-Chapter Sketch*
6. *Author's Bio*
7. *Sample Material*

A sample *Proposal Package* follows.

> *"Creativity can solve almost any problem. The creative act, the defeat of habit by originality, overcomes everything."*
> — George Lois

# Sample Non-Fiction Proposal Package

CORN SUGAR AND BLOOD
Rick Porrello

OVERVIEW

When "Big Joe" Lonardo and his three brothers settled in Cleveland, they were followed here by the seven Porrello brothers, boyhood friends from Licata, Sicily. "Big Joe," backed by a fierce gang, eventually controlled much of the bootleg-related crime in northeast Ohio. Joe Porrello was a corporal in Lonardo's gang.

In 1925, Porrello left the Lonardos and organized his brothers who became corn sugar dealers like the Lonardos. When the Lonardos obtained a lock on the sugar business, they had only one competitor. You guessed it, their old friends the Porrellos.

Soon after "Big Joe" Lonardo left on a long trip to Sicily, the Porrellos began taking over Lonardo customers, growing prosperous and powerful in a short time. When "Big Joe" returned, a former Lonardo employee took advantage of the stormy situation and set up "Big Joe." His murder shocked the underworld and started a bitter campaign of revenge by the Lonardo family. In the process, another Lonardo brother was killed and four of the seven Porrello brothers died. This story was the bloodiest chapter in organized crime between Chicago and New York and made front-page headlines for five years. It is still featured occasionally in magazine and newspaper articles.

RESEARCH

I am a suburban Cleveland police officer and have been researching this story for over three years. Having grown accustomed to the raised eyebrows and wise guy comments, I now feel fortunate to admit that this fascinating piece of history is part of my family background. You see, my grandfather and his six brothers are among the main characters. I also feel fortunate to be the first person able to tell the story in its entirety.

With the exception of an unexpected need for further information, research for CORN SUGAR AND BLOOD has been completed. At my present pace, the story should be completed by the first months of 1993. Book length is estimated at 80,000 to 90,000 words. I have a collection of over 120 photographs available, many of which have never been viewed before by the public.

ABOUT THE AUTHOR

Rick Porrello is a Greater Cleveland police officer with Mafia roots. His grandfather and three uncles were mob leaders killed in Prohibition-era, bootleg violence. Porrello is an accomplished musician, having spent almost three years traveling worldwide as the drummer for the late Sammy Davis, Jr. Rick has a degree in criminal justice. He is married and lives in suburban Cleveland.

**THE RISE AND FALL OF THE CLEVELAND MAFIA -
CORN SUGAR AND BLOOD
CHAPTER-BY-CHAPTER SYNOPSIS**

Chapter 1
Birth of the Cleveland Mafia

During the late 1800s, the four Lonardo brothers and seven Porrello brothers were boyhood friends and fellow sulphur mine workers in their hometown of Licata, Sicily. They came to America in the early 1900s and eventually settled in the Woodland district of Cleveland. They remained close friends. Several of the Porrello and Lonardo brothers worked together in small businesses.

Lonardo clan leader "Big Joe" became a successful businessman and community leader in the lower Woodland Avenue area. During Prohibition, he became successful as a dealer in corn sugar, which was used by bootleggers to make corn liquor. "Big Joe" provided stills and raw materials to the poor Italian district residents. They would make the booze and "Big Joe" would buy it back, giving them a commission. He was respected and feared as a "padrone" or godfather. "Big Joe" became the leader of a powerful and vicious gang and was known as the corn sugar "baron." Joe Porrello was one of his corporals.

Chapter 2
The First Bloody Corner

With the advent of Prohibition, Cleveland, like other big cities, experienced a wave of bootleg-related murders. The murders of Louis Rosen, Salvatore Vella, August Rini, and several others produced the same suspects, but no indictments. These suspects were members of the Lonardo gang. Several of the murders occurred at the corner of E. 25th and Woodland Ave. This intersection became known as the "bloody corner."

By this time, Joe Porrello had left the employ of the Lonardos to start his own sugar wholesaling business. Porrello and his six brothers pooled their money and eventually became successful corn sugar dealers headquartered in the upper Woodland Avenue area around E. 110th Street.

With small competitors, sugar dealers, and bootleggers mysteriously dying violent deaths, the Lonardo's business flourished as they gained a near monopoly on the corn sugar business. Their main competitors were their old friends the Porrellos.

Raymond Porrello, youngest of the brothers, was arrested by undercover federal agents for arranging a sale of 100 gallons of whiskey at the Porrello-owned barbershop at E. 110th and Woodland. He was sentenced to the Dayton, Ohio, Workhouse.

The Porrello brothers paid the influential "Big Joe" Lonardo $5,000 to get Raymond out of prison. "Big Joe" failed in his attempt but never returned the $5,000.

Meanwhile, Ernest Yorkell and Jack Brownstein, small-time, self-proclaimed "tough guys" from Philadelphia, arrived in Cleveland. Yorkell and Brownstein were shakedown artists, and their intended victims were Cleveland bootleggers, who got a chuckle out of how the two felt it necessary to explain that they were tough. Real tough guys didn't need to tell people that they were tough. After providing Cleveland gangsters with a laugh, Yorkell and Brownstein were taken on a "one-way ride."

## Chapter 3
## Corn Sugar and Blood

"Big Joe" Lonardo, in 1926, now at the height of his wealth and power, left for Sicily to visit his mother and relatives. He left his closest brother and business partner John in charge.

During "Big Joe's" six-month absence, he lost much of his $5,000-a-week profits to the Porrellos, who took advantage of John Lonardo's lack of business skills and gained the assistance of a disgruntled Lonardo employee. "Big Joe" returned and business talks between the Porrellos and Lonardos began. They "urged" the Porrellos to return their lost clientele.

On October 13, 1927, "Big Joe" and John Lonardo went to the Porrello barbershop to play cards and talk business with Angelo Porrello, as they had been doing for the past week. As the Lonardos entered the rear room of the shop, two gunmen opened fire. Angelo Porrello ducked under a table.

Cleveland's underworld lost its first boss as "Big Joe" went down with three bullets in his head. John Lonardo was shot in the chest and groin but drew his gun and managed to pursue the attackers through the barbershop. He dropped his gun in the shop but continued chasing the gunmen into the street where one of them turned and, out of bullets, struck Lonardo in the head several times with the butt of his gun. John fell unconscious and bled to death.

The Porrello brothers were arrested. Angelo was charged with the Lonardo brothers' murders. The charges were later dropped for lack of evidence. Joe Porrello succeeded the Lonardos as corn sugar "baron" and later appointed himself "capo" of the Cleveland Mafia.

## Chapter 4
## The Cleveland Meeting

The trail of bootleg blood continued to flow with numerous murders stemming from the Porrello-Lonardo conflict.

Lawrence Lupo, a former Lonardo bodyguard, was killed after he let it be known that he wanted to take over the Lonardo's corn sugar business.

Anthony Caruso, a butcher who saw the Lonardos' killers escape, was shot and killed. It was believed that he knew the identities of the gunmen and was going to reveal them to police.

On December 5, 1928, Joe Porrello and his lieutenant and bodyguard Sam Tilocco hosted the first known major meeting of the Mafia at Cleveland's Hotel Statler. Many major Mafia leaders from Chicago to New York to Florida were invited. The meeting was raided before it actually began. Joe Profaci, leader of a Brooklyn, N.Y., Mafia family, was the most well-known of the gangsters arrested. He was the founder of the Colombo Mafia family. Vincent Mangano also ranked high as founder of the Gambino family, most recently headed by the "Dapper Don" John Gotti.

Within a few hours, to the astonishment of police and court officials, Joe Porrello gathered 30 family members and friends who put up their houses as collateral for the gangsters' bonds. Profaci was bailed out personally by Porrello. A great controversy over the validity of the bonds followed.

Several theories have been given as to why the meeting was called. First, it was thought that the gangsters, local presidents of the Unione Siciliane, an immigrant aid society infiltrated by the Mafia, were there to elect a new national president. Their previous president Frankie Yale had been recently killed by order of Chicago's notorious Al Capone. Second, it was believed that the meeting may have been called to organize the highly lucrative corn sugar industry. It was also said that the men were there to "confirm" Joe Porrello as "capo" of Cleveland.

Capone, a non-Sicilian, was reported to be in Cleveland for the meeting. He left soon after his arrival at the advice of associates who said that the Sicilians did not want him there.

Chapter 5
The Second Bloody Corner

As Joe Porrello's power and wealth grew, heirs and close associates to the Lonardo brothers grew hot for revenge.

Angelo Lonardo, "Big Joe's" 18-year-old son along with his mother and his cousin, drove to the corner of E. 110th and Woodland, the Porrello stronghold. There Angelo sent word that his mother wanted to speak to Salvatore "Black Sam" Todaro. Todaro, now a Porrello lieutenant, had worked for Angelo's father and was believed to be responsible for his murder. In later years, it was believed that he was actually one of the gunmen.

As Todaro approached to speak with Mrs. Lonardo, whom he respected, Angelo pulled out a gun and emptied it into "Black Sam's" stocky frame. Todaro crumpled to the sidewalk and died.

Angelo and his cousin disappeared for several months, reportedly being hid in Chicago courtesy of Lonardo friend Al Capone. Later, it was believed that Angelo spent time in California with his uncle Dominick, the fourth Lonardo brother who fled west when indicted for a payroll robbery murder in 1921.

Eventually, Angelo and his cousin were arrested and charged with "Black Sam's" murder. For the first time in Cleveland's bootleg murder history, justice was served as both young men were convicted and sentenced to life. Justice, although served, would be short-lived as they would be released only a year and a half later after winning a new trial.

Chapter 6
Rise of the Mayfield Road Mob

On October 20, 1929, Frank Lonardo, brother to "Big Joe" and John, was shot to death while playing cards. Two theories were given for his death: that it was in revenge for the murder of "Black Sam" Todaro; and that he was killed for not paying gambling debts. Mrs. Frank Lonardo, when told of her husband's murder, screamed, "I'll get them. I'll get them myself if I have to kill a whole regiment!"

By 1929, Little Italy crime boss Frank Milano had risen to power as leader of his own gang, "The Mayfield Road Mob." Milano's group was made up in part of remnants of the Lonardo gang and was also associated with the powerful "Cleveland Syndicate," Morrie Kleinman, Moe Dalitz, Sam Tucker, and Louis Rothkopf. The Cleveland Syndicate was responsible for most of the Canadian booze imported via Lake Erie. In later years, they got into the casino business. One of their largest and most profitable enterprises was construction of the Desert Inn Hotel/Casino in Las Vegas. Dalitz would become known as the "Godfather of Las Vegas." He would be murdered in 1986 as part of a Mafia war for control of Las Vegas.

Joe Porrello admired Milano's political organization, the East End Bi-Partisan Political Club, and, seeing the value in such influence, wanted to ally himself with the group. Milano refused. Later, Porrello was reported to have affiliated himself with the newly formed 21st District Republican Club. He hoped to organize the Woodland Avenue voters as Milano was doing on Mayfield Road.

Chapter 7
More Corn Sugar and Blood

By 1930, Milano had grown quite powerful. He had gone so far as to demand a piece of the lucrative Porrello corn sugar business. On July 5, 1930, Porrello received a phone call from Milano who had requested a conference at his Venetian Restaurant on Mayfield Road. Sam Tilocco and Joe Porrello's brother Raymond urged him not to go.

At about 2:00 p.m., Joe Porrello and Sam Tilocco arrived at Milano's restaurant and speakeasy. Porrello, Tilocco, and Frank Milano sat down in the restaurant and discussed business. Several of Milano's henchmen sat nearby. The atmosphere was tense as Porrello refused to accede to Milano's demands.

Porrello reached into his pocket for his watch to check the time. Two of Milano's men, possibly believing that Porrello was reaching for his gun, opened fire. With three bullets in his head, Porrello died instantly. Simultaneously, a third member of Milano's gang fired at Tilocco, who was struck three times but managed to stagger out the door toward his new Cadillac. He fell to the ground as the gunmen pursued him, finishing him off with another six bullets.

Frank Milano and several of his restaurant employees were arrested but only charged with being suspicious persons. The gunmen were never actually identified. Only one witness was present in the saloon when the shooting started. He was Frank Joiner, a slot machine distributor whose only testimony was that he "thought" he saw Frank Milano in the restaurant during the murders.

Cleveland's aggressive and outspoken Safety Director Edwin Barry, frustrated by the continually rising number of bootleg murders, ordered all known sugar warehouses to be padlocked. He ordered a policeman to be detailed at each one to make sure that no sugar was brought in or removed.

Meanwhile, the six Porrello brothers donned black silk shirts and ties and buried their most successful brother. The showy double gangster funeral was one of the largest Cleveland had ever seen. Two bands and 33 cars overloaded with flowers led the procession of the slain don and his bodyguard. Over 250 automobiles containing family and friends followed. Thousands of mourners and curious onlookers lined the sidewalks.

Cleveland's underworld was tense with rumors of imminent warfare. Porrello's brother Vincente-James spoke openly of wiping out everyone responsible for his brother's murder.

Three weeks after his brother's murder, Jim Porrello still wore a black shirt as he entered the I & A grocery and meat market at E. 110th Street and Woodland. As he picked out lamb chops at the meat counter, a Ford touring car, its curtains tightly drawn, cruised slowly past the store. A couple of shotguns poked out and two thunderous blasts of buckshot were fired, one through the front window of the store and one through the front screen door.

The amateur gunmen got lucky. Two pellets found the back of Porrello's head and entered his brain. He was rushed to the hospital.


Chapter 8
"I think maybe they'll kill all us Porrellos."

"I think maybe they'll kill all us Porrellos. I think maybe they will kill all of us except Rosario. They can't kill him - he's in jail." Thus, Ottavio Porrello grimly but calmly predicted the probable fate of him and his brothers as he waited outside Jim's hospital room.

Next to Ottavio was a tough looking young man who smoked cigarettes and blew the smoke at the hospital's No Smoking signs. It was said he was a bodyguard, something the Porrellos never employed enough of. Jim Porrello died at 5:55 p.m.

Two local petty gangsters were arrested and charged with murder. One was discharged by directed verdict, and the other was acquitted. Like almost all of Cleveland's bootleg-related murders, the killers never saw justice.

About this time, it was rumored that the Porrello brothers were marked for extermination. The surviving brothers went into hiding. Raymond, known for his cocky attitude and hot temper, spoke like his brother James did of seeking revenge. Raymond was smarter though, he took active measures to protect himself.

On August 15, 1930, three weeks after James Porrello's murder, Raymond Porrello's house was leveled in a violent explosion. He was not home at the time, since he had taken his family and abandoned his home in anticipation of the attack.

Four days later, Frank Alessi, a witness to the murder of "Big Joe" Lonardo's brother Frank, was gunned down. From his deathbed, he identified Frank Brancato as his assailant. Brancato was known mainly as a Lonardo supporter and suspect in several murders. Brancato was acquitted of Alessi's murder.

Chapter 9
This shooting was Cleveland's deadliest Mob hit ever.

In March of 1931, Rosario Porrello was paroled from Ohio's London Prison Farm where he had served one year for carrying a gun in his car.

In mid-1931, National Mafia "capo di tutti capi" (boss of all bosses) Salvatore Maranzano was killed. His murder set in motion the formation of the first Mafia National Ruling Commission, created to stop the numerous murders resulting from conflicts between and within Mafia families and to promote application of modern business practices to crime.

Charles "Lucky" Luciano was the main developer of the commission and was named chairman. Also named to the commission were Al Capone of Chicago, Joe Profaci of Brooklyn, and Frank Milano of Cleveland.

In December of 1931, Angelo Lonardo and his cousin Dominic Suspirato were released from prison after being acquitted of "Black Sam" Todaro's murder during a second trial. Because he had avenged his father's death and (for the most part) gotten away with it, he became a respected member of Frank Milano's Mayfield Road Mob.

The thirst for revenge had not been satisfied for members of the Lonardo family. It was generally believed that "Black Sam" Todaro instigated and perhaps took part in the murders of "Big Joe" and John Lonardo. However, it was believed by members of the Lonardo family that the remaining Porrello brothers, particularly the volatile John and Raymond and eldest brother Rosario, still posed a threat because of the murders of Joe and James Porrello.

On February 25, 1932, Raymond Porrello, his brother Rosario, and their bodyguard Dominic Gulino (known also by several aliases) were playing cards near E. 110th and Woodland Avenue. The front door burst open and, in a hail of bullets, the Porrello brothers, their bodyguard, and a bystander went down. The Porrellos died at the scene. Gulino died a couple of hours later. The bystander eventually recovered from his wounds. This shooting was Cleveland's deadliest Mob hit ever.

Several hours after the murders, Frank Brancato, with a bullet in his stomach, dragged himself into St. John's Hospital on Cleveland's west side. He claimed he was shot in a street fight on the west side. A few days later, tests on the bullet taken from Brancato revealed that it came from a gun found at the Porrello brothers' murder scene. Although never convicted of either of the murders, Brancato was convicted of perjury for lying to a Grand Jury about his whereabouts during the murder. He served four years after a one- to ten-year sentence was commuted by Governor Martin L. Davey.

In 1933, Prohibition was repealed. The bootleg murders mostly stopped as organized crime moved into other enterprises. Angelo Lonardo continued his crime career as a respected member of the Cleveland family, eventually rising through the ranks to run the northeast Ohio rackets in 1980.

Chapter 10
"Big Ange" and the Death of the Cleveland Mafia

In 1983, Angelo Lonardo, 72, one-time Cleveland Mafia boss, turned government informant. He shocked family, friends, law enforcement officers, and, particularly, criminal associates with his decision, which was made after being sentenced to life plus 103 years for drug and racketeering convictions. The sentence came after a monumental investigation into the murder of the greatly feared Mafia enemy Danny Greene. The complex plot to kill "The Irishman" involved Mafia members from, and associated with, Erie, New York, Youngstown, Akron, and the West Coast.

"Big Ange" as he was called, was the highest ranking mafioso to defect. He testified in 1985 at the Las Vegas casino "skimming" trials in Kansas City and in 1986 at the New York Mafia "ruling commission" trials. Many of the nation's most powerful mob leaders, including Tony Salerno, boss of the Genovese crime family, were convicted as a result of these trials.

# The Submission Package for Adult Fiction

## Elements of a Submission Package for Adult Fiction

The following must be included in a submission package for a book of adult fiction:

1. A Title Page
2. A Table of Contents
3. A Synopsis
4. A Chapter-by-Chapter Sketch
5. An Author's Bio or Curriculum Vitae
6. Sample Material

A sample synopsis follows on the next page.

# The Submission Package for Children's Books

## Elements of a Submission Package for a Children's Book

1. A Title Page
2. A Table of Contents for the Submission Package
3. An Author's Bio
4. A One-Page Description of Potential Markets
5. Your Completed Manuscript

*"When love and skill work together, expect a masterpiece."*
John Ruskin

# Sample Synopsis

Places the Dead Call Home
By Paul L. Hall

Synopsis

On a summer night in 1958, bullets tear through the body of a young man on a lonely Oklahoma highway. Nineteen years later, a soldier lies in the pool of his own blood on an army base in Virginia. Death has made room at home for both of them. Death can always find room for more.

Josh Kincaid is a common link to both events. In 2002, when Kincaid's cousin proposes an urgent trip to the Anasazi ruins of Mesa Verde to resolve the riddle of one of these deaths, Kincaid reluctantly agrees. Soon, he and a van full of misfits are on the way to the cliff dwellings of the "ancestral enemies," where flesh-and-blood enemies await them among the ruins.

This sets the stage for Places the Dead Call Home.

Josh Kincaid is happy with life in Phoenix where he manages a bar and sells a few drugs on the side  His serenity is soon shattered, however, by a call from his cousin, Frankie McKnight, who claims to know why Josh's father died many years earlier far from his Detroit home in the parking lot of a gas station in Oklahoma City.

General Herman Endicott is looking for Josh, too. The highlight of his military life was winning the Silver Star for bravery in Vietnam, followed a few years later by his promotion to General. But between those events, the death of a friend and the betrayal of an old comrade have brought disgrace to a bereaved widow and her unborn child. This secret could destroy the General, and Josh Kincaid may know that secret.

General Endicott hires Tommy Three Hands, an Indian living in the Phoenix area, to kill Josh and Frankie, along with a reporter named Jeffrey Bonus and his traveling companion, Jeanette Koskos, who have also shown up with questions about the death of Bonus's father. Tommy is an ex-con who distrusts and hates whites, enjoys a reputation for violence and betrayal, and has a cruel streak when it comes to women. He also has a grudge against Josh and his cousin Frankie.

All of these characters converge on Mesa Verde, where the secret of the mysterious—and perhaps violent—disappearance of the Anasazi still seems to inhabit the ruins.  As Josh and Frankie seek the answer to Jimmy Kincaid's destiny in the park's mythic heritage and Bonus hopes to learn the true fate of his father, Tommy and the General are making plans of their own to ensure that the dead stay where they belong—the places they call home.

*6. A Sample Illustration, if you choose to include one*

The first four elements of the submission package for a children's book you've already reviewed. And, as you can see, no synopsis, book proposal, or chapter-by-chapter sketch is included. The inclusion of any of the above would be foolish. The inclusion of the entire manuscript should speak for itself.

### INCLUDING A SAMPLE ILLUSTRATION

Only include a sample illustration if you are capable of either illustrating your book yourself or if you already have an artist whom you plan to use. Please also be aware that only an 8 1/2" x 11" black-and-white sample illustration needs to be included. In addition, you should also know that less than half of the potential children's book publishers accept outside illustrators. Most prefer to use their own. Thus the literary agents you are submitting to may be cool on the idea as well. But don't let this deter you if you are either bound and determined to illustrate your own book, or if you have an artist outside of the publishing industry you are determined to work with.

*"Music is my mistress and she plays second fiddle to no one."*
Duke Ellington

# Preparing to Create the Submission Package – An Energy and Timesaving Exercise

The first rule in composing a submission package is that you have to make your educated, professional readers FEEL that what you have to offer is worthy of their time, and at the same time aid them in understanding the potentialities of your project. To do this can seem an insurmountable task. In fact, no other activity has caused my students more strife. However, I have a solution for dealing with that dilemma.

I find that all those who come to me, after going through the exercises at the beginning of this book, receive a vision or an image in their mind, one of great completeness, which offers all that they need to know to understand the thrust of, and reason behind, their desires to write. Communicating this under the pressure of it being reviewed and judged as a submission package by literary agents is another thing altogether.

In the vast majority of cases, the pressure upon even the finest writers was far too great. They literally cracked, some unable to write at all. Many never made it beyond this point. Those who did oftentimes had to work through dozens of drafts to regain their well-formed literary voices, which had been avalanched by their overreactions to the situation.

I knew that there had to be an easier way around this dilemma, something that would enable them to retain their literary voices and complete the necessary work smoothly and efficiently. It was

> *"I'm going to turn on the light, and we'll be two people in a room looking at each other and wondering why on earth we were ever afraid of the dark."*
> Gale Wilhelm

> "He is rich or poor according to what he is, not according to what he has."
> — Henry Ward Beecher

during one of my lectures on the exact topic that the inspiration came to me.

Why not have them form the basis for writing their synopsis or proposal, the components they struggled with the most, by composing a letter to a close friend, with whom they obviously would feel very comfortable.

Yes, that was it! It had been a long-recognized fact that we have always done our finest writing when communicating with someone that we know and trust. If we simply approached a close and dear comrade with a letter describing what we wanted to do and how we were going to do it, not only would our most natural of all voices flaunt itself, but the style would only have to be altered slightly to become the synopsis or proposal that we wanted it to be.

The technique worked so well that I have been using it ever since, saving aspiring writers dozens of useless drafts and, in the most extreme cases, keeping the vast majority of those I work with from giving up in the face of the rigors of this step.

To best activate this technique, get in a deep relaxed state. Upon opening your eyes, begin your letter with the words, *"Dear..., I have a great idea for a book."*

Then take off. Let your passions for your idea be your guide. Empty yourself onto the paper. Leave no stone unturned. Act as if it has been a substantial time since you have last spoken to your friend and that he or she knows nothing about your idea.

Describe how the book idea came to you. If it's fiction, describe who the characters are; if it's non-fiction, who you think will buy it and how it would best be promoted. Mention why you feel that you are the best writer to author this story. Empty your soul onto paper. Let it all hang out.

In the following sample, just such a letter has

been included. Remember it is very rough and doesn't in any way showcase the author's exceptionally refined ability. But, hopefully, from reading it, you will grasp the understanding behind this unique, brainstorming, idea-formulating technique.

*"Human salvation lies in the hands of the creatively maladjusted."*
Martin Luther King

# Sample Brainstorming Letter

Dear Tom,

    I have a great idea for a book about when people learn to think reflectively. From my years in the classroom, I learned that when students think superficially and do not get involved with the task, they score poorly. A good memory will get students high scores on multiple-choice tests without the benefit of really learning or understanding much. Students learn to play the game of school, sometimes spending more time avoiding involvement than it would take to learn the lesson. These students, and I think they are the majority, graduate from high school with little reading and writing practice, getting by with doing as little as possible. Although they may or may not go to college, they are not lifelong learners. I call these passive learners "aliterates" because although they are able to decode and encode, it is in the area of comprehension that their thinking skills are lacking.

    Actually, I want you to know that this is not only my opinion; the National Assessment of Educational Progress has found plenty of evidence. In fact, the great school reform movement in the late 80s was a direct result of these test scores, which revealed that students could read and write, but they were not very good at thinking. If you remember, there were several books concerned with education on the bestseller list. You probably remember *Cultural Literacy, Frames of Mind, Among Schoolchildren, High School, The Closing of the American Mind*. Responses to these publications indicate that there is presently a national concern for teaching and learning in American schools.

    Unfortunately, I have to add that my work at the college level with student teachers and their cooperating teachers has given me reason to believe that many teachers are not "thinkers" either. Kids need role models. "Do as I say, not as I do," doesn't work well. Recently I read a book by Howard Gardner entitled, *The Unschooled Mind* (1991), which really made an impression on me. Anyway, Gardner writes, "Children read not because they are told — let alone ordered to read, but because they see adults around them reading, enjoying their reading, and using that reading productively for their own purposes, ranging from assembling a piece of apparatus to laughing at a tall tale." I am convinced that this is true, not only when it comes to reading, but also, to thinking.

    There is one more thing I want to mention that brought me to the point of thinking that I could write a book about thinking. You see, I have been thinking about thinking for some time now. The term educators use when they discuss "thinking about thinking" is metacognition, which means that a person can be aware of his own thinking processes. In other words, I'm sure you have talked to yourself or questioned your own motives for doing something. I tell my student teachers that it is one thing to recall the lesson or to describe what the kids did, but they have an added benefit if they think about the students' perspective, or what they could have done differently, or if time could have been spent more wisely. I heard a teacher say once, "Boy, the whole class did poorly on that test. Those kids must not have studied;" the idea that it may have been a "poor" test never entered the teacher's mind.

    Secondly, along the same line, I have done a great deal of research on writing. I wrote my dissertation on writing, I go to conventions on writing, I attend seminars on writing, and occasionally, I do writing workshops for English teachers. My doctoral degree is in language communications, and I am well aware of the theoretical and practical approaches to teaching and learning reading and writing. Furthermore, everything that I have been reading lately connects writing to thinking.

The last thing I need to bring up is what teachers refer to as Bloom's Taxonomy of Educational Objectives, which describes six levels of cognition. The levels are 1) knowledge – recall information, 2) comprehension – summarize or paraphrase, 3) application – relate to a prior experience, 4) analysis – classify, categorize, compare parts, 5) synthesis – put together in a new way, and 6) evaluation – make informed judgments and support opinion. Originally, the taxonomy was thought of as a hierarchy, meaning that you had to teach at level one before going to level two, but today it is used as a simple way to look at how thinking skills are related to teaching and learning. However, there is plenty of research to indicate that what we teach in schools is mainly lower-level thinking, tasks that require recall and paraphrase at the knowledge and comprehension levels. Generally, we think of application, analysis, synthesis, and evaluation as higher-order thinking skills. Perhaps this is another reason that students score poorly on higher-level thinking skills.

The good news is, we do know how to teach and learn these skills. It seems to me that most of us reach a point in time when we realize that it is important to think clearly, or at least we see a need for being a better thinker. How many times have you said, "I just didn't think." The drunk driver has said it. The inexperienced hunter has said it. Young mothers have said it. Probably, the Vice-President has said it. Habits of thinking can be improved quite easily. For example, if your child complains about an assignment at school, ask him what the teacher could have done to make it a better learning experience, or, if your child wants to write a letter to the editor of a newspaper because bicycles aren't allowed on sidewalks, take a moment to have him think about other points of view — the elderly who may not see well, parents of small children, or homeowners liable for injuries on their property.

To tell you the truth, Tom, I read a book once and I quit smoking. I read a book and I got organized. I read a book and I made a quilt. Last week there was an article in the *Wall Street Journal* about entrepreneurs who began with a "How To" book. Why not a book about thinking?

Boni

## SENDING YOUR SUBMISSION PACKAGE

After your submission package has been completed, you want to send it first to the one or two agents you are interested in least. Then be patient. If you get an offer of representation from one of your first submissions, then send your packages out to the remaining agents. Allow up to eight weeks for them to respond before replying one way or another to the initial offer. If you don't receive an offer of representation from your first submissions, check out the turndown letters for reasons why you were not offered a contract. Is there anything you can change to make your package more saleable? If so, alter such before resubmitting to your other sources.

Aggressively follow this strategy until all your literary agents have been contacted and you have at least one offer to represent you. If you run out of sources, query some other agencies, and constantly improve your material if you feel that it needs it.

## DECIDING UPON A LITERARY AGENT

If you are fortunate enough to have more than one literary agency offer you representation, which is what this entire system has been designed to do, think long and hard about which representative you choose to go with. Call the agencies and ask them any questions or express any hesitancies you may have before making your decision. After you've made your decision and have properly informed

*"Imagination is more important than knowledge."*
— Albert Einstein

your choice, contact your other final candidates, explaining what agency you went with and why. Make sure that you don't burn any bridges with the finalists whom you didn't choose. Make sure that the door is open to reapproach them in the future if, for some reason, your relationship with the agent you did choose doesn't work out.

## Commonly Asked Questions About Submitting Your Writing

*How long do you have to submit your submission package after getting a positive response from an agent?*

It is of the utmost importance that your submission package be a good representation of both you and your idea. How long it will take to get it there is up to you. Simply inform your interested sources when you feel that you will be able to get your package to them. Unless yours is a very timely piece, and the chances are small that it will be, they are usually more than happy to work with you. At the same time, it shows a significant amount of efficiency on your end if you politely keep them abreast of your progress on a monthly basis. It also doesn't allow them to lose you in the maze of writers that contact them on a daily, weekly, and monthly basis.

*Should you have your material bound before submitting it?*

The addition of a plastic spiral binding may seem to add an aura of professionalism to any submission. But it is not a necessity, nor is it expected

> "Creative activity could be described as a type of learning process where the teacher and pupil are located in the same individual."
>
> Arthur Koestler

> "I'm at the age where I think more about food than sex. Last week I put a mirror over my dining room table."
> — Rodney Dangerfield

by those who will be on the receiving end of your submission. In fact, there are some literary sources that detest spiral bindings because they make access to your work much harder for photocopying and distribution to their colleagues.

*How long should a synopsis or proposal be?*
Neither has any presupposed length. Each should simply and thoroughly introduce your idea, telling all that needs to be told, as gone over earlier, to fully enlighten your sources to the depth, width, and potentiality of your project.

*How much do you have to pay a literary agent?*
If a literary agent charges you any more than a commission of between 10-15%, plus expecting you to reimburse them for reasonable out-of-pocket expenses (long distance costs, mailing expenses, and any typing or copying costs, if necessary), there's an excellent chance that you are dealing with a less than worthy source. In that case, stay clear of that person. Their inability to properly market books has probably led them to seek an income in less than honest ways.

*What should I do when an agency asks to review my material on an exclusive basis?*
Do not in any way deceive an agency in thinking you are giving them an exclusive shot at your work when you're not. Just arrange your submission strategy to accommodate their request. Or even better, you can guarantee an agency asking for an exclusive look that you will not select any other agency for representation before hearing back from them, as long as they reply in a timely fashion of no more than three weeks after receipt. That seems most fair to both parties.

Above all, it's important to be honest at all times.

# Chapter Eight: Literary Agent Agreements

Because of the important role your literary agent will play in your eventual success, the contract you will sign with him or her is the most important contract you will sign in your young writing career. There are only three types of agreements that one can enter into with a literary agent. Here they are, listed from the worst to the best.

## A Time-Related Agreement

A time-related agreement basically states that any and all works that you compose will be the sole responsibility of a specific literary agent to market over a certain period of time, usually two years. Though this sort of agreement greatly benefits a literary agent, it is the worst possible contractual relationship of this type that you can enter into. The reason is simple: You will be giving away all the representative rights of all your works for a sig-

*"One way to get high blood pressure is to go mountain climbing over molehills."*
Earl Wilson

nificant period of time to an agency who you cannot guarantee is the best to handle your work. And if you have made a mistake in your decision to go with a certain agency, who pays most for the mistake? You do, via lost opportunities, in addition to having to potentially buy your way out of such an agreement if you do discover that the agent you chose is not the right one for you.

## A Project-Related Agreement

Project-related agreements carry a significant amount of liability on your end as well, but not nearly as much as its time-related counterpart.

A project-related agreement states that you are allowing a literary agency to solely handle the representative rights to a specific project or projects. But what happens if the literary agent you signed on with under this sort of design doesn't turn out to be the right one for you? You may have to buy your way out of your agreement with your representative to take your project to another literary agent.

There is a way to make this sort of agreement very livable. Simply make sure that somewhere it is stated in your contract that if your book project is not sold within a certain period of time (usually one year is very fair), for an acceptable amount, then you can choose to cancel your agreement with your literary agent at no cost. This will allow you to be able to go somewhere else without having to pay your former literary agent for any job they were unable to do.

## Open-Ended Agreements

An open-ended contract is the best agreement that you can hope for, because it allows you to cancel your commitment with a literary agent at any

*"The high prize of life, the crowning fortune of a man, is to be born with a bias to some pursuit which finds him in employment and happiness."*
Emerson

time with no penalty to you. Varieties of this sort of agreement range from verbal agreements to typical written agreements.

# OTHER CONTRACTUAL CONSIDERATIONS

## EXPENSES

If a literary agent charges you expenses outside of mailing costs, typing costs (if needed), and copying costs (if needed), they are probably getting some sort of kickback from the expenditures. True, honest, and sincere literary agents derive their incomes only from the commissions via sales of books. If a literary agent has to charge for extremely padded expenses, they're probably not doing their job. If that's the case, what does that tell you? Right. They're not a very good salesperson, which is their primary function to you, and, thus, probably not the right literary agent for you or anyone else.

## HIDDEN COSTS

The bottom line is that if a literary agent tries to rope you into a contract that obligates you to pay for editing fees, rewriting fees, consultation fees, or anything like these, they're not worth your time. Again, like those who over-emphasize expenses, and probably severely pad them, they're probably not bringing in enough commission to support themselves and their business, so they turn to less honest means to acquire their income. Literary agents who hit you with hidden costs are not only not worth your time, but could prove to be extremely dangerous to your career. Avoid these people.

*"What a wonderful day we've had. You have learned something, and I have learned something. Too bad we didn't learn it sooner, we could have gone to the movies instead."*
Balki Bartokomous,
*Perfect Stranger*

# Sample Literary Agreement

THE ETHAN ELLENBERG LITERARY AGENCY
AGENCY AGREEMENT

AGREEMENT made between TOM BIRD _____ of _____, (hereinafter referred to as "You") and THE ETHAN ELLENBERG LITERARY AGENCY, of 548 Broadway, 5-E, New York, NY 10012, (hereinafter referred to as "I") dated March 6, 2004.

1. TERM. This agreement shall commence immediately upon execution of this contract and shall continue in full force, until terminated by either party upon written notice to the other.

2. WORKS COVERED. During the term of this agreement, I shall be your sole and exclusive agent for all your literary properties, including books, screenplaysk and dramatic plays. For works that I secure a publisher, I shall have the right to receive the commissions specified in this agreement for additional rights sold while this contract is in effect, and I shall also be entitled to such commissions even if this agreement has terminated. To such end I will normally control the unsold rights to a property I have placed, though on termination of this agreement, these terms will be subject to negotiation between the parties.

Should I choose not to handle a work, I shall give you a written release for such work, and you shall be free to sell rights to it, without any compensation to me. However, no such event shall terminate or impair this exclusive agreement.

3. COMPENSATION. In return for all services rendered, I shall receive an irrevocable share and interest of FIFTEEN (15%) PERCENT of gross monies received and to be received by you for the placement of any domestic rights to a property, FIFTEEN (15%) PERCENT of gross monies for the placement of any performance or dramatic rights for a property, and TWENTY (20%) PERCENT for the placement of any foreign rights for a property, it being understood that for foreign rights I shall often be employing a sub-agent in the country where such rights are being placed.

4. EXPENSES. The direct costs incurred by the agency on the author's behalf shall be billed and promptly paid by the author as incurred. Such expenses shall include the cost of copying manuscripts, postage, bank fees, purchase of finished copies for the sale of subsidiary rights, and postage for the shipment of such copies to the buyers of subsidiary rights both in the U.S. and in foreign markets. The Author shall not be liable for any other costs, and extraordinary expenses must be approved by the author prior to their being incurred.

5. SERVICES RENDERED. I agree to render the following services:

• Review manuscripts

• Negotiate sale or lease of rights to the Works, including translation and performance rights

• Collect monies due and promptly render you your share

- Examine royalty statements

- Check on publisher's performance

- Check on copyright

- Timely notification on the status of properties.

    It is understood that I am not an attorney, not a tax, legal, or business consultant, and I have no obligation to render any such services under this agreement.

    6. This agreement represents the complete agreement between the parties and can only be modified in writing. It shall be binding on the heirs, executors, successors, and assigns of both parties. It shall be governed under the laws of the State of New York.

Sincerely,

ETHAN ELLENBERG

_____

ACCEPTED AND AGREED:

_____

TOM BIRD

# Chapter Nine: Contractual Obligations
## for Shorter Pieces

Literary agents normally don't represent shorter pieces. There's just not enough money in it for them. Thus, with shorter pieces, in most cases, the sale of your work is directly between you and the magazine(s) you are dealing with.

Once a source decides that they will accept your article, short story, etc., for possible publication, then it is time to negotiate a contract.

## Getting It in Writing

Get all of the agreed-upon contractual arrangements in writing before submitting your work. There are three ways to do so.

> 1. *Via the use of a written, legal contract. If you plan to do a lot of this work, it would be to your advantage to have your attorney*

*"The only man who is really free is the one who can turn down an invitation to dinner without giving an excuse."*
— Jules Renard

> *"The only true happiness comes from squandering ourselves for a purpose."*
> — William Cowper 1731-1800

*draw up a simple agreement that you could adapt to the specifics of your situation.*

2. *Through a confirming letter sent to you by your source confirming all the specifics that you agreed to.*

3. *By a confirming letter, listing all the specifics agreed upon, sent by you to your source, which your source acknowledges with his or her signature at the bottom of the correspondence and then returns to you.*

# Elements of a Magazine Contract

Following are the elements that need to be agreed upon in a magazine contract.

## Money

With the exception of well-known magazines with substantial circulations that offer a very rewarding standard fee to their writers, how much you will be paid is determined by a few different factors: the size and budget of the publication you are dealing with, how badly they may want your piece, your credentials, and, most of all, your confidence when negotiating your fee.

Basically, a publication with a tight budget will offer you the least amount of money they feel that you will accept to write a piece. So don't be afraid to say *"No"* to their first offer. In fact, in dealing with such publications, it's not a bad negotiating practice to routinely say *"No"* to each offer you receive until you can receive an offer that is fair.

## WHETHER YOU WILL BE WRITING ON ASSIGNMENT OR SPECULATION

Writing on speculation simply means that a magazine will agree to pay you only after seeing a completed piece and accepting it for publication. If they like it, you'll get paid what you agreed upon. If not, maybe they'll give you another chance to do it over. But then maybe they won't.

Writing on assignment means that a publication will commit to your piece without seeing it first, though this luxury is usually reserved for the proven writer.

## KILL FEE

A kill fee is a specific percentage of the money a publication has agreed to pay you for a piece if, for some reason, your work is not published by an agreed-upon date. I usually agree to nothing lower than a 50% kill fee. This means if I sell an article for $1,000, and the magazine that I contracted with doesn't run my article by a specific date, I will be paid $500 for the piece and its rights returned to me.

## PAYMENT SCHEDULE

In the world of magazines, there are only two ways that you are paid, either on acceptance or upon publication. Of course, being paid once your material is accepted is always best. But that right is often reserved only for the seasoned or experienced writer. Being paid upon publication means that you won't be issued a check until after your work appears in print, which means that you may not see any money until months after you've actually finished writing a piece.

*"The method of the enterprising is to plan with audacity, and execute with vigor; to sketch out a map of possibilities; and then to treat them as probabilities."*
—Bovee

> *"I was going to buy a copy of The Power of Positive Thinking, and then I thought: what the hell good would that do?"*
> — Ronnie Shakes

## Expenses

Make sure to discuss being reimbursed for any out-of-pocket expenses you may run into when working on a piece. This is an area which many writers sorely neglect, and, thus, they net a lot less on their writing than they could have.

## Photographs

Oftentimes publications are unwilling to pay the rates of a freelance photographer, so often a deal hinges on whether you, the writer, are capable of providing accompanying photographs. Make sure to negotiate an additional fee up-front before doing so. In almost every case, you will be paid well.

## Length

The agreed-upon length of a piece determines how severely a magazine can alter your work without your permission. For example, let's say that you agreed to write a 2,000-word article and just before your publication date an aggressive salesperson at the magazine makes a last-minute sale of some advertising space. The magazine would just love to chop out 300 words of your article to make room for the ad, but they can't unless they consult you first. Of course, if you didn't have this clause in your agreement, they could chop all they wanted, literally mutilating your work. Who would look bad? You. Your name is on the article. The proper inclusion of this clause prohibits that nightmare from happening.

# Contractual Obligations for Shorter Pieces

## Delivery

This area of any contract simply states when you will have your piece to a magazine.

## Publication Date

Agreeing upon exactly when your piece will be published keeps a magazine from procrastinating in regards to printing your piece. It also ensures that you will be paid at an agreed-upon time and guarantees your material can be sold elsewhere if the magazine you've contracted with doesn't publish your work by the predetermined date.

## Rights

There are three types of rights that you need to consider when negotiating the placement of a piece. The first type is *First North American Rights*, which allows a publication to print your piece before anyone else in the country. That's it. After that, the rights revert back to you, and you can do what you please with the material.

The second type of rights are *Resale Rights*. These are utilized only after you have already sold your First North American Rights. As I'm sure you would expect, resale rights are usually less valuable than First North American Rights.

The third type involves the selling of *Exclusive* or *All Rights* to a publication. This means that they can do primarily what they want with the piece. If they sell it to be used somewhere else, it's OK, as long as they give you your byline.

Of course, if you involve yourself in this third type of situation and sell All Rights, you should be compensated even better than you would have been for the sale of your First North American Rights. Usually, in a situation such as this, a writer is com-

> *"The thing always happens that you really believe in; and the belief in a thing makes it happen."*
> Frank Lloyd Wright

pensated up to four times as much as he or she would have gotten for his or her First North American Rights or is paid a percentage, anywhere between 50-75%, of any further monies earned from the eventual sale of the piece.

That's it.

Just remember: In dealing with a magazine, always get any deal in writing and never start writing until your signed, written agreement has been received.

*"Never give in. Never. Never. Never. Never."*
                    Sir Winston Churchill

# Informal Magazine Agreement

January 4, 1992
Mike Mason
44 Hargrove Dr.
Westport, Michigan 97863
313-555-2343


Roger Wright, Editor
Airline Magazine
1222 Blvd. of the Americas
New York, New York 10010

Dear Roger,

It is with great pleasure that I write this letter in regard to Airline Magazines commissioning of my piece entitled Above The Rest. As we discussed on the 27th of last month, I am confirming that I will be producing the 2,000-word article on a speculation basis and will have the work to you no later than April 5, 2004. If the work meets with your satisfaction, a decision will reach me no later than April 30, 2004. I will be paid $750 for the First North American Rights of the article, plus any incidental expenses such as mailing costs, long-distance costs, etc.

As well, we agreed that I will be paid upon publication of the work, which is scheduled for no later than your December issue of this year. If for some reason, after accepting the material, you cannot use it by that time, I will still be paid a 50% kill fee, and the First North American Rights will revert back to me.

In addition, as per your request, I will be more than happy to provide the accompanying photos for the article. As you requested, I will provide you with two completed rolls of Kodachrome 25 by April 30, 2004. Your magazine will be responsible for the processing and developing of the film. If my article is accepted, I will not only be reimbursed for the cost of the film, but paid $150 for each photo that I took which is used in your magazine. If you choose not to use my article, I will still be reimbursed for the cost of the film, all the negatives and accompanying photos will be returned to me, and I am free to sell their First North American Rights elsewhere.

This concludes all that we agreed upon. All rights not herein granted are reserved to me, and this letter when signed by both of us will constitute our agreement. Any amendments to it must be made in writing and agreed upon by both of us.

Sincerely,
_____
Mike Mason

_____
Roger Wright

# FORMAL MAGAZINE AGREEMENT

AGREEMENT

This agreement made as of the _____ of _____, _____, by and between _____ of _____, _____(hereinafter referred to as AUTHOR), and _____ of _____ Magazine (hereinafter referred to as MAGAZINE).

WHEREAS, the AUTHOR agreed to provide on speculation, for the purpose of a First North American Rights publication, a _____ word article, currently titled _____ _____, to MAGAZINE by _____, _____.

THE MAGAZINE agrees to review the AUTHOR'S submission as quickly as possible and contact the AUTHOR with a final decision in regards to publication no later than _____. If, at that time, the MAGAZINE decides not to publish the AUTHOR'S work, then the MAGAZINE shall return all copies of the above to the AUTHOR within ten (10) working days, and all rights will revert immediately to the AUTHOR.

IF, HOWEVER, THE MAGAZINE AGREES TO PUBLISH THE AUTHOR'S WORK, the AUTHOR will be paid $800, plus any expenses up to $200, for the article within thirty (30) days of the MAGAZINE'S publication of the above. As well, the AUTHOR agrees to provide one roll of KodaCOLOR 25 film on the above topic to the MAGAZINE by _____, _____, for which the AUTHOR will be paid _____ apiece for any of AUTHORs photographs that are published by the MAGAZINE.

AS WELL, the MAGAZINE agrees to publish the AUTHOR'S article no later than _____, _____. If for whatever reason after accepting the AUTHOR's article by _____, _____, then the AUTHOR shall be paid a kill fee of 50%, be reimbursed for all out-of-pocket expenses, plus the cost of the roll of KodaCOLOR 25 film, and all copies of the AUTHOR's work and photographs shall be returned to him within ten (10) working days from the date listed above in this paragraph and all rights to the above shall return to the AUTHOR.

THIS AGREEMENT, which constitutes the entire understanding of the parties, may be amended or modified only in writing signed by both parties, and shall be governed by the laws of the Commonwealth of _____.

IN WITNESS WHEREOF, the parties hereunto have set their respective hands and seals as of the day and year first above written.

_____    _____
WITNESS:                               AUTHOR

_____    _____
WITNESS:                               MAGAZINE

# Step Five:
# The Sale Phase 5

**Goal for Books:**
**To Receive an Offer From a Publisher**

**Goal for Shorter Pieces:**
**To Receive an Offer to Purchase Your Work**

## Some More Good News

"Were it not for his valuable insight and input, my book would not be the book it is today, and possibly wouldn't even have been written...." Deborah Tyler Blais, <u>Letting Your Heart Sing</u>

"I just got a phone call from Llewellyn, and they want to publish my teen goddess book! Contract is in the mail. I am so happy I could fly!!!! Now I have to start writing my next book!" Catherine Wishart, <u>Teenage Goddess: How to Look, Love, and Live Like a Goddess</u> (Llewellyn)

"Even Stephen King could learn something from taking one of Tom's courses." Jean Marie Stine, <u>Writing Successful Self-Help & How To Books</u>

"Thanks again for getting me excited about starting one of my lifelong dreams." Mike C., Georgia

"With a highly contagious, 'go for it' attitude, Tom Bird and his informative series of books are an excellent guide and best friend for the author-to-be." Rick Porrello, <u>The Rise and Fall of the Cleveland Mafia</u> (Baracade Books)

# Introduction

If you have made it this far, congratulations. If you still have not sent out that query letter, what are you waiting for?

This is the simplest of all the steps, so simple is this step that, frankly, all you need to do is keep from screwing up all that you have accomplished so far and you will be there. Please keep that in the forefront of your mind, and you will enjoy the sweet taste of publication which you seek.

Godspeed.

---

*"Everyone is necessarily the hero of his own life story."*
John Barth

# Chapter Ten: The Sale

## Longer Material

Having garnered the representation of a well-known literary agent and having your book taken to the marketplace is a very exciting event, but the work doesn't stop there. There are still three basic activities you are responsible for during this step.

First, the great excitement and exhilaration of this phase breeds great emotion all across the board, which, if not properly channeled, could cause rampant confusion, doubt, and frustration. The confusion and doubt come in response to your great success and fortune. Yes, there is a downside. In most cases, we have a difficult time believing that what is happening to us, that which we wanted for so long, has appeared at all, let alone so fast. As a result, thoughts of doubt start to dominate our minds.

*"I haven't heard from (agent) today. I wonder if*

> *"We may allow ourselves a brief period of rejoicing."*
> Sir Winston Churchill, on the Day WWII ended

all is going well? Maybe all the publishing houses that my book was sent to turned us down. Yeah, and maybe he's (or she's) just frightened to tell me. Maybe I had better give him (or her) a call."

"Hey, I've got a great idea that I think will make my book even more marketable. I know the stuff is already out to the publishing houses, but I think that I'll give (agent) a call anyway."

"Hummmm, let's see, what reason could I use today to give (agent) a call? I don't want to be a pain in the butt, so I had better think of something. I mean, I don't want to call and just bug him (or her) about the book. Let's see what excuse did I use yesterday, because I don't want to use the same one today? Oh yeah, I remember now. Well, maybe today I'll use the one about the chocolate cake I know he (or she) likes. I'm quite a cook and I could..."

"(Agent) said he (or she) would have my book sold by today. Or at least I think that's what he (or she) said. Well, it's not sold, damn it. I think it's about time that I call and give that son of a gun a piece of my mind. I'm not going to be seconded to any client. I don't care who it is. I'll show this son of a gun who he (or she) is dealing with. He's (or she's) going to get a piece of my mind. Probably just needs a good kick in the butt. Well, I'll show him (her)."

"I know that it's after midnight, but I just can't sleep. This whole sale thing is just driving me crazy. I need to be reassured. I'm sure that (agent) won't mind if I call. That's why he (or she) gave me his (or her) home number anyway, isn't it?"

I'm sure you get the idea. No matter how refined you are in most circumstances, because of the impact of this sort of arrangement and situation, there's an excellent chance that you may become unwound, and in doing so, you could ruin and then dissolve the valuable relationship that you waited so long for and worked so hard to acquire.

> *"Why do they call them tellers? They never tell you anything. They just ask questions. And why do they call it interest? It's boring. And another thing – how come the Trust Department has all their pens chained to the table?"*
>
> Coach Ernie Pantusso, "Cheers"

To prevent yourself from experiencing this form of self-sabotage, I strongly suggest that you set up some sort of communicative routine with your agent where he or she checks in with you via phone, e-mail, or fax every 3–4 weeks, and then stick to it. Don't let your fears, worries, doubts, and concerns get the better of you. Using the above technique, you will be receiving the timely updates that you deserve, while you'll be giving your agent the time, space, trust, and freedom that he or she needs to do the job.

Employing a system such as this and sticking to it, will pay off for you in spades. Your agent will appreciate your professionalism and will reward you by being able to devote more of his or her energy to the sale of your work. Your sane and professional approach will also make you stand out favorably from the other clients that he or she represents. As a result, you will get better service all the way around, and he or she will be able to boast about you to the potential purchasers of your work as a model client, which goes very, very far in today's high-pitched, crazy, emotional world of publishing.

Second, use the time while your work is being shopped to study the following material on publishing agreements. By doing so, not only will you be preparing yourself to understand and then make the proper decisions when your contract comes through, but you will be sending out good vibes to yourself, as well.

The third and probably most important step that you can take to benefit yourself, your agent, and the eventual elevation of your goals as a writer, is to begin on a second book. I know that your logical mind is probably telling you that doing so is crazy. *"I mean, shouldn't I wait until the first one is sold before I go wasting time on working on another one?"*

> *"If your parents didn't have any children, there is a good chance that you won't have any."*
> Clarence Day

No. Go ahead and start work on that next project now. You'll have to just take my advice here. But, toss the following back at your old logical mind to see if these rock-solid reasons for doing so will better ease its concerns.

The first reason that you begin work on a second project is in hopes that you will become so distracted with it that you will better be able to give your agent the time, space, and freedom he or she needs to best complete the sale of your work.

Also, your second book will be better than your first and, as a result, may have a better chance of selling. In fact, in my estimation, my students' second works are usually at least three times as well written as their first works. The reason for this is because so much time and energy (I estimate 85% of your available time and energy) is expended learning to write on your first book that there is little time left to address the actual inspiration as it comes through you. That reverses with your work on the second book, which can't help but make your work a more powerful read.

Third, you begin work on your second book at this time because you're a writer and writers write. We're not professional telephone watchers who just sit around hours upon hours waiting for our agents to call, even though you may be hard pressed to find an agent that would agree with me on that point.

Another reason to begin work on your second book is because you're probably already in good writing shape, and you might as well take advantage of it.

Lastly, the final reason for doing so is because having a second or third or fourth or whatever project ready to go to market just provides you with that many more opportunities to succeed. Remember the primary point in this section, though. Make yourself different. Make yourself

*"All human activity is prompted by desire."*
Bertrand Russell

special. Conduct yourself professionally, and you'll be amazed with the results.

In this industry, the squeaky wheel doesn't get greased, it gets replaced if it squeaks too often, especially if it is a brand new wheel.

*"The real secret of success is enthusiasm."*
Walter Chrysler

# BOOK PUBLISHING AGREEMENTS

As specified much earlier in this book, here are the primary components of a publishing agreement that would be best for you to be aware of.

Remember, you are ultimately responsible for any contract you sign. So, it's best to fully understand all of the necessary elements of that contract before doing so. It's not fair to either you or your agent if you leave the decisions that will affect you and your career so deeply up to him or her.

## AN ADVANCE AGAINST ROYALTIES EARNED

An advance against royalties earned is more commonly referred to just as an *advance,* and is defined as *risk money against potential royalties earned.* It is what your publisher hopefully will be offering you. It is the dollar figure authors continually refer to when they talk about how much money they have received for their books. So you will fully understand this very important point, let me illustrate for you what an advance is and how it works.

Bob receives a $10,000 advance. When released, his book will sell for $20. Bob is to be paid a 10% royalty rate on the cover price of every book sold. Thus he makes $2 per book sold. How many of Bob's books does his publisher have to sell before Bob makes back his advance? Right – 5,000 books.

After that, he begins to earn a per-copy royalty on all further books sold, which his publisher pays semi-annually.

What if Bob's book doesn't sell enough copies to make back his advance? Is he responsible for returning any portion of his advance not covered by book sales?

Technically, yes, he is responsible for covering the remaining amount. But rarely, unless the low sale is the result of his direct actions, does a publisher ever ask you to do so. Plus, to legally force you to do so would cost them much more than they would ever be able to gather from you.

## Payment of an Advance

Though they can take almost any form, advances are either paid in two or three payments. If paid in two payments, half of the advance is usually given upon the signing of a book contract, and the second half is received after the manuscript has been delivered. On the three-payment system, one-third is received upon the signing of an agreement; the second third is sent out after the first half of the manuscript has been delivered; and the last third is paid once the remainder of the manuscript has been completed.

## Royalties

Royalties are paid in two ways. First, they can be paid upon the actual cash received by the publisher, which can be anywhere from a 35-45% discount off the cover price of the book. Or secondly, they can be paid on the actual list price of the book, a vast difference. Obviously, the latter alternative will earn you significantly more than the former.

Standard hardback royalties are calculated on

*"Good people are good because they've come to wisdom through failure."*
— William Saroyan

a 10% rate on the first 5,000 copies of a book sold; 12-1/2% on the next 5,000 sold; and 15% on all copies sold beyond 10,000.

Paperback royalties range from a 5-8% royalty rate up to the first 30,000 copies sold, and 10% from that point forward. Of course, how much you eventually make all depends upon whether a publisher publishes the paperback edition in-house or sells it to another house to have it done. See Paperback Considerations below for further explanation.

*"After a time, you may find that having is not so pleasing a thing, after all, as wanting. It is not logical, but it is often true."*
Spock,
*"Star Trek"*

## DEADLINE

This is the consideration that most new writers innocently squirm over most. But don't allow yourself to fret over being able to make your deadline. Publishers usually deal very fairly in this regard. They certainly are not the browbeaters that unknowing writers and a misled public make them out to be. A publisher usually discusses with you when they would ideally like a book completed and are very open to your realistic abilities.

## COPYRIGHT

The publisher handles for you the copyrighting of your manuscript in your name.

## PAPERBACK CONSIDERATIONS

If your publisher sells the paperback rights of your hardback book to another publishing house, they are usually entitled to a standard cut of 50% of anything you make from the softcover sale of your book. If they publish your paperback edition in-house, they receive no extra percentages or fees, and you receive your agreed upon royalty rate.

### Book Club Rights

If your publishing house sells the rights of your work to a book club, they receive a standard 50% of all monies you earn.

### Subsidiary Rights

As with the two categories listed directly above, your publishing house receives a standard 50% of all monies earned from the sale of subsidiary rights. For example, if your publisher sells a first serial excerpt of your book to a major magazine, which pays $20,000 for the piece, you will receive a $10,000 check, minus your agent's fee, based upon the typical 50-50 split.

### Foreign Rights

If your publishing house sells the foreign rights to your work to another firm, it is standard that you will be expected to turn over 50% of monies earned from your foreign sales to your publisher. If the house you contract with publishes your book in-house for foreign consumption, you will not be expected to share 50% of all monies you earn with your publisher. In such a case, you will just receive a standard royalty rate.

### Movie Rights

Since most publishing houses do not specialize either in the sale or production of movies, it is in the best interest of you and your literary representative to retain these rights.

---

*"Faith is the bird that feels the light and sings when the dawn is still dark."*
　　　　Rabindranath Tagore

# Articles, Short Stories, and Poetry

LISTEN. That's right. LISTEN. That is your major objective to accomplish in this phase with your shorter material. For if you LISTEN, you will learn. If you learn, you will understand; if you understand, you will grow; and if you grow, you will succeed. But it all begins with LISTENING.

The people that you will be listening to are your prospective editors. These people will potentially offer you suggestions. But they will only do so if they see potential in you and your work, and their comments will help you reach that potential. That doesn't mean that you should take their advice verbatim, but you would be missing a huge opportunity to grow and succeed faster if you were not to LISTEN. Whatever you do with their suggestions is up to you. But LISTEN, for this industry will teach you everything that you need to learn if you just do that. Why wouldn't you LISTEN in the first place?

Because all of us have been hurt at one time or another during our lives in response to creatively expressing ourselves. The greater the amount of time between when that initial blow took place and now, the greater the defensiveness on our end. It's that defensiveness that could keep us from hearing what it is that could benefit us the most. Don't allow that to happen to you. Shrug off the past, close your mouth, open your ears, and LISTEN. If you are asked to take into consideration some suggestions to improve your work, do it. That doesn't mean that you have to adhere to anything. But LISTEN. You may just learn something which will serve to greatly contribute to the speed and breadth of your eventual success.

*"It is the supreme art of the teacher to awaken joy in creative expression and knowledge."*

Albert Einstein

# Commonly Asked Questions

*How long will it take for my book to be sold?*

That all depends on several factors (the aggressiveness and knowledge of your literary agent, the quality of your material, the mindset of the publishing industry at the time of your submission), most of which are out of your control.

The best way to answer this question for yourself is to ask your literary agent's opinion on how long it will take your material to be sold. Do this before you sign a contract with him or her, and this will help you gauge how aggressive they plan to be.

*How much can I expect to make on my first book?*

That varies greatly depending upon the above factors and the type of material that you are writing. However, when books of all types are taken into consideration, the average advance for the first-time author in hardcover usually pans out to around $10,000, coupled with the standard royalty rates of 10% on the first 5,000 copies sold; 12-1/2% on the second 5,000; and 15% on any books sold over 10,000. But it has been my experience that writers using this system usually receive twice the average advance for their fiction and over three times as much for their non-fiction.

*Should I use a pen name?*

The name that you choose to put on the cover of your work is totally up to you. The only time it is necessary to use a pen name is when you deliberately want to hide your affiliation with a project because another book or two will be available close together, such as in the case of a romance book author releasing two new works at the same time.

---

*"Literature is news that stays news."*

Ezra Pound

*How beneficial are writing groups?*

Because they are run by well-meaning but unsuccessful writers, most groups of this sort do more to hurt than to help you. If you can find a group that is headed by a successful, knowledgeable, and egoless published writer, you will probably have found a fertile place to learn, grow, and succeed. If not, there are plenty of books on the shelves that would help you much more than the typical writers group, which often does more to bring you down than lift you up.

*How long will it take for me to get published?*

The answer to that question is completely subjective and depends totally on you. However, if you move swiftly and confidently, you should be able to breeze through the first two steps in one to two months for the shorter pieces and four to six months for books. How long the process will take from there depends upon the aforementioned, extraneous factors.

*Can I really make a living doing this?*

Definitely! In fact, with the ever-expanding media markets, there has never been a better time to be a writer than today. Also, writing is one of those rare professions that doesn't place any weight on your age, sex, sexual preference, education, color, or socioeconomic background. If you can write, want to write, and are willing to endure the emotional upheavals you may put yourself through with the submission of your work, you have what it takes to make it in this business.

*How much money will it take me to become an author?*

Money isn't much of a factor here. Sure, you should have a computer, and it's a good idea if you take a class or two. Then there are costs for mailing

"Literature and butterflies are the two sweetest passions known to man."
Vladimir Nabokov

and paper and such. But outside of that, writers pay for their successes with the sweat of their souls. The monetary investment is small, but the emotional output is great.

You'll never be the same after embarking on your writing career. You'll just keep getting better and better and happier and happier as you go.

*"Suffering is not a prerequisite for happiness."*
Judy Tatelbaum

## A Closing Note

All that has been standing in your way up to this point is the will to move forward and the proper techniques and strategies to do so. The latter has been offered to you through this book  The rest is up to you. GO FOR IT!

# APPENDIX

## Other Books and Software by the Author

*Willie Stargell,* with Willie Stargell (Harper & Row, 1984)

*How To Get Published* (Sojourn, 1986)

*KnuckleBALLs,* with Phil Niekro (Freundlich Books, 1986)

*Literary Law* (Sojourn, 1986)

*Beyond Words* (Sojourn, 1987)

*POWs of WWII: Forgotten Men Tell Their Stories* (Praeger, 1990)

*Fifty-Two Weeks or Less to the Completion of Your First Book* (Sojourn, 1990)

*The Author's Den* interactive computer program (Sojourn, 1993)

*Hawk,* with Andre Dawson (Zondervan, 1994)

*Hawk,* the children's version (Zondervan, 1995)

*Get Published Now!* (Sojourn, 2001)

*~~Write~~ Right From God* (Sojourn, 2002)

*Your Artist Within* (Sojourn, 2004)

*Tom Bird's Selective Guide to Literary Agents* (Sojourn)

# APPENDIX

## PUBLICATIONS WHERE THE AUTHOR'S WORK HAS APPEARED

A prolific writer, as well as teacher of writing, Bird's own work has appeared in dozens of notable journals including:

*Parade*
*USA Today*
*Popular Mechanics*
*New Writer's Magazine*
*Vegetarian Times*
*The American Banker*
*Racquetball Illustrated*
*Racquetball Everyone*
*Racquetball*
*Strength and Health Magazine*
*The Pittsburgh Post Gazette*
*Pittsburgh Magazine*
*Cleveland Magazine*
*Nautilus Magazine*
*Austin Magazine*
*Baseball America*
*Sail*
*Steeler Weekly*
*Erie Magazine*
*Erie Times News*

## Venues Where the Author Has Presented His Ideas

Tom Bird has shared his vision with tens of thousands of writers during more than 900 speaking appearances at more than 90 colleges, universities, and workshops from coast to coast and border to border, including:

Duke University
College of William and Mary
University of Texas
Florida Atlantic University
Temple University
University of Tennessee
Ohio State University
University of Nebraska
University of New Mexico
Penn State University
University of Arizona
University of Missouri
University of North Carolina
Memphis State University
Nova University
University of Florida
University of Cincinnati
University of Pittsburgh
Florida State University
Emory University
New York State University
University of Nevada – Las Vegas
Northern Arizona University
Florida International University
University of New Mexico
Louisiana State University
University of North Florida
Slippery Rock State University
Augusta State University
Central Florida University
University of Central Florida
Queens College

Robert Morris College
Mercyhurst College
Santa Fe Community College
The Chautauqua Institute
Scottsdale Community College
Seton Hall College
Butler County Community College
Allegheny County Community College
John Tyler Community College
J. Sargent Reynolds Community College
Paul D. Camp Community College
Com. College of Cuyahoga County
Lakeland Community College
Beaver Valley Community College
Pima County Community College
Tidewater Community College
Colin County Community College
Mesa Community College
Paradise Valley Community College
Yavapai Community College
St. Petersburg Community College
Youngstown State University
Valdosta State University
Niagara University
Edinboro University
Indiana State University
Old Dominion University
Panama City Community College
San Diego State University
The Sedona Arts Center

# APPENDIX

## TELEVISION AND RADIO APPEARANCES

Mr. Bird is familiar to radio and television audiences due to dynamic presentations on his work and his appearances on such high-profile national television and radio shows as *The David Letterman Show, The Tonight Show, CBS Morning News, The Today Show, The Charlie Rose Show, CBC,* and *The 700 Club.* Highlights include:

### RADIO

WBVP – Beaver, PA
WBUT – Butler, PA
WDAD – Indiana, PA
WDSY – Pittsburgh, PA
WJET – Erie, PA
WGLU – Johnstown, PA
WLTJ – Pittsburgh, PA
WORD – Pittsburgh, PA
WPIT – Pittsburgh, PA
WQED – Pittsburgh, PA
WQLN – Erie, PA
WTAE – Pittsburgh, PA
WWSW – Pittsburgh, PA
WHRO – Norfolk, Va
KDKA – Pittsburgh, PA
WGN – Chicago
WOR – New York
KQV – Pittsburgh, PA
WBCN – Boston
WSBR – Boca Raton
WJMK – Chicago
WBZ – Boston
WODS – Boston
KNBR – San Francisco
KGO – San Francisco
WFVD – New York
KMOX – St. Louis
KOST – Los Angeles
Moody Press Line – Chicago
WHYY – Philadelphia
WAXY – Miami
KEX – Portland, OR

### TELEVISION

The David Letterman Show
The Tonight Show/Johnny Carson
The Today Show
CBS Morning News
Pittsburgh Today
Cleveland Today
The Charlie Rose Show
CBC
The 700 Club
WGN - Chicago
WTAE – Pittsburgh
KDKA – Pittsburgh
WOOR – New York
WMC – Memphis
WCFC – Chicago
WPIX – New York
WHDH – Boston
KMOX – St. Louis
KRON – San Francisco
WAVY – Norfolk
WPGH – Pittsburgh
WPXI – Pittsburgh
WEWS – Cleveland
KTVU – Oakland
WSVN – Miami
WICU – Erie, PA
WJET – Erie, PA
WSEE – Erie, PA

# Newspapers That Have Featured the Author's Work

Prescott Daily Courier
Pasadena Herald & Tribune
Wheeling Intelligencer
Verde Valley News
Orange County Register
Los Angeles Times
Long Beach Gazette
Oakland Tribune
Pasadena Star News
Riverside Press
San Diego Union-Tribune
San Francisco Chronicle
San Francisco Examiner
Jamestown Post-Journal
Hartford Advocate
Washington Post
New York Daily News
Valdosta Daily News
Chicago Sun-Times
Boston Globe
Boston Herald
Gloucester Daily Times
Oak Park Journal
Publishers Weekly
Kirkus Reviews
The Library Journal
Detroit Free Press
Tupelo Daily Journal
Sporting News
Baseball Digest
Baseball America
Omaha World Herald
Newark Star-Ledger
Dallas Morning News
Houston Chronicle
Berkley Register Herald
Fairmont West Virginian
Martinsburg Journal
Weirton Daily Times
Coraopolis Record
Cranberry Journal
Wheeling News Register
Portland Oregonian
The Toronto Sun
The Toronto Star
Beaver County Times
Bridgeville Area News
Parkersburg Sentinel

DuBois Courier Express
Erie Times News
Erie Morning News
Brown-Thompson Newspapers
Irwin Standard Observer
McKeesport Daily News
Oklahoma City Journal Record
North Hills News Record
Atlanta Journal-Constitution
Philadelphia Inquirer
Philadelphia Daily News
Pittsburgh Post Gazette
Pittsburgh Tribune Review
USA Today's Baseball Weekly
Tarentum Valley News Dispatch
Washington Observer-Reporter
Cincinnati Enquirer/Post
Cleveland Plain Dealer
Columbus Dispatch
Santa Barbara News-Press
Memphis Commercial Appeal
Steubenville Herald Star
St. Louis Riverfront Times
Chautauqua News
Newport News-Hampton Daily
Norfolk Virginian-Pilot
Portfolio Magazine
Richmond Times-Dispatch
New Writer Magazine
Carolina Beach Weekly News
Charlotte Observer
Greensboro News and Record
Nags Head Sentinel
Daytona Beach News-Record
Fort Lauderdale Sun-Sentinel
Sarasota Herald-Tribune
St. Petersburg Times
Tallahassee Democrat
Jacksonville Fla. Times-Union
Huntington Herald Dispatch
Morgantown Dominion Post
Red Rock News
Red Rock Review
Long Island Newsday
The Montreal Gazette
Bradford Era
Butler Eagle
Millcreek Sun

USA Today
Buffalo News
Standard Observer
Sewickley Herald
Sharpsburg Herald
Pittsburgh Press
New York Post
New York Times
Boca Raton News
Bradenton Herald
Gainesville Sun
The Miami Herald
Orlando Sentinel
Tampa Tribune
Daily Sun
Meadville Tribune
Indiana Gazette

# ORDER FORM

## BOOKS AND PROGRAMS OFFERED BY TOM BIRD
15% OFF When Ordering Through
www.TheSpiritOfPublishing.com

### YOUR ARTIST WITHIN
This book shows you how to make the ultimate of all connections and to live your life's purpose. For the aspiring author, it also shares a system for completing a book in 45 days or less. Price $27.00 / **SALE $24.00**.

### TOM BIRD'S 2004 SELECTIVE GUIDE TO LITERARY AGENTS DATABASE
The ultimate consumer's guide for the aspiring author looking to land the right literary agent. Newly updated, this year's edition boasts over 400 of the industry's top literary agents. Organized as a computer database, this unique version allows you to access your chosen sources with a click of your mouse and to merge them all together, saving you days of precious time when submitting query letters. (E-mailed to you after purchase.) Price $39.00 / **SALE $33.00**.

### THE SPIRIT OF PUBLISHING: The Ultimate Guide for Getting Whatever It Is That You Write Into Print Now!
Recently revised and updated, this mainstay of Tom's teaching offers you absolutely everything that you will need to see your work in print, no matter what it is that you want to write. Plenty of winning examples given, including query letters and submission packages. Price $29.00 / **SALE $25.00**.

### WE DO THE WORK FOR YOU
Tom will review your query letter once, then, after your approval, we'll e-mail the query for you. All the responses will come direct to you and your computer. Quick, simple, easy. Price $115.00 / **SALE $97.75**.

### PURCHASE ALL THREE FOR EXTRA DISCOUNTS:
The Spirit of Publishing: How to Get Your Writing into Print Now!, Your Artist Within; and the Agent's Database, all for $82.00 / **SALE $74.00**.

**Ordering Information:** S&H $5.00 for 1-2 books, $6.00 for 3. Arizona Residents, please add 7% Sales Tax. Please make your checks out to: Tom Bird Seminars, Inc. and mail to, P. O. Box 4306, Sedona, AZ 86340. Or, fax Visa, MC, Discover, or AMX credit card information to 928/203-0264. Online Ordering is also available through PayPal.

For further information, feel free to either give us a call at 928/203-0265 or visit our website at http://www.TheSpiritOfPublishing.com

**All Major Credit Cards Accepted.**

(Prices subject to change without notice.)

Printed in the United States
17145LVS00002B/79-82